THE ONE THING I WANT YOU TO KNOW

LIFE LESSONS TO LIVE BY

24 Sept. 2023

Dear Marcia.

You, yourself, so full of wisdom... I can't wait to receive your insights. The world is igno-rant. Only TRUE stories can cause

INSPIRED WORLD PUBLISHING

the change required.

♥ with love Margaret

CONTENTS

INTRODUCTION

"One day you will tell your story of how you've overcome what you're going through now, and it will become part of someone else's survival guide." ~ Brene Brown

---

When I came up with the theme for this book I knew I wanted it to be an opportunity for the authors to share their compelling stories and unique wisdom to help others.

Storytelling is powerful. I know that personally I've felt so much comfort, hope, inspiration and motivation from reading other people's stories.

And stories that share important lessons are even more impactful.

When I've shared my personal stories and the lessons I've learnt from them I've had people reach out to me to thank me, to share their own stories and to connect with me.

As a PR strategist I've helped my clients to share their stories and wisdom in media outlets across the globe, reaching millions of people who have benefitted from knowing that they're not alone, that there's light at the end of the tunnel, and that if this person has gone through this and come out stronger, they can too.

And of course they've used these opportunities to connect with potential clients, meaning they're creating a bigger impact in the world whilst growing their business.

I've personally shared stories and lessons around the challenges of dealing with my Dad's mental health issues over the years, and how I learnt that talking about what it's like to have a parent with mental health problems can help other people going through something similar.

I've shared stories around finding my voice, overcoming Imposter Syndrome, and finally learning to speak up.

I've shared the story of the heartbreak I felt at unexpectedly being let go from my job as a magazine journalist, and the challenge of making a full time living as a freelance journalist, and how learning how to effectively pitch the press changed everything.

I've shared stories about the difficulties I faced when I first started out in business and found myself overworked and underpaid and heading for burnout, and how I overcame that by shifting my mindset and finally seeing myself as an expert and then getting visible and putting myself out there.

So when I started planning this book, I was clear that it would offer a chance for the authors to share their stories of hope, inspiration and motivation as well as the lessons they've learnt from them.

"The One Thing I Want You To Know: Life Lessons To Live By" is an anthology featuring life lessons from nine inspirational women from across the globe, who are each experts in their fields.

They have shared their biggest life lessons, and what they've learnt from them, alongside practical tips and advice to help you understand how to improve different areas of your own life.

The authors have pulled back the curtain on their personal journeys and the challenges and adversities they've overcome. And they've shared takeaways from the lessons they've learnt, alongside their wisdom and knowledge.

Their stories are truly inspiring and motivating, and their wisdom and insight will help you to improve your own health, wealth and happiness.

Their personal accounts include everything from overcoming mental illness, stress and burnout, to healing after bereavement and the aftermath of suicide, to journeying through spiritual awakenings, dealing with relationship breakdowns and divorce, career reinvention, finding your voice, amongst others. These stories will take you on a journey - some may make you cry, others will make you smile and laugh.

Each chapter also features tips and advice that will help elevate your home life, work life, health, relationships and more.

This book will leave you feeling truly inspired and motivated, as well as offering practical life lessons that you can apply to your own life for increased happiness, better health, improved relationships and more financial success.

Enjoy their stories, learn from their wisdom and if the authors have touched you in any way, please reach out to me or them to let us know. We wish you happiness, health and wealth, and a lifetime of beautiful stories and lessons.

Dina Behrman

PR Strategist and Publisher at Inspired World Publishing

Find out more at www.dinabehrman.com

1

ABIGAIL MENSAH-BONSU

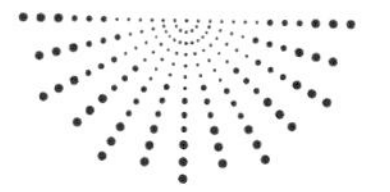

UNVEILING THE PATH OF DHARMA

The path winds and twists,
unyielding and unknown,
a journey of the soul,
where the heart finds its home.

Amidst the trials and tests,
we search for our way,
seeking truth and purpose,
with each step, come what may.

The journey may be perilous,
the way may not be clear,
but with an open heart and mind,
the path begins to appear.

Through the veil of uncertainty,
we catch a glimpse of light,

guiding us forward,
through the darkness of night.

The path of Dharma unfolds,
revealing destiny and fate,
as we embrace our truest selves,
a world of wonder awaits.

With every step forward,
we release the past and pain,
embracing our deepest purpose,
our lives never the same.

The journey of the soul,
unveils moments great and small,
as we find the path of Dharma,
our heart responds to the call.

One thing I have learned in my life is that this journey we are on is that of the soul and it's not meant to be a straight line.

Our soul paths unfold while we are living life. One day we wake up in our element, and we realize that we are doing exactly what we are here to do. It is not known from the beginning, but our soul path makes itself known as we continue to take the steps showing up, doing what we are here to do and what lights us up.

During my journey through college, I passionately pursued pre-med and psychology in order to realize my lifelong dream of becoming a medical doctor. Given that both of my parents are nurses, I was immersed in the medical field at an early age and developed a deep reverence for the human body. What set me apart was my innate ability to intuit when I was about to become ill and locate the root cause within my body. Knowing how to restore balance to my system, I heeded my body's requests and craved foods that would deliver what it needed, such as vividly-colored oranges and verdant greens rich in vitamin C. Having strengthened my immune system, I was able to keep sickness at bay.

Motivated by my burning desire to enlighten people about the power of self-healing, I embarked on the path of becoming a medical doctor, believing that it would be the most effective way to achieve my goal.

To fulfill my aspirations, I diligently fulfilled all the necessary pre-medical requirements and successfully completed the MCAT (Medical College Admission Test) exam during my college years. In my junior year, I eagerly took up the opportunity of shadowing medical doctors to gain firsthand insight into what their professional life entailed. The entire experience turned out to be an exciting and enjoyable process.

During one particular week of my medical shadowing experience, I had the opportunity to observe two doctors closely- one male and one female. I made a deliberate effort to select doctors of each gender. On the day I was following the male doctor, he posed a question that every pre-med student is required to answer at some point: "Why do you want to become a doctor?" Without hesitation, I eagerly shared my deeply held belief that I wanted to teach people how their bodies had the ability to heal themselves.

He laughed and I smiled. He said "That would be amazing but you would not be able to do that in the medical field."

His unexpected response took me aback, leaving me perturbed. He explained to me that the medical field had strict laws, rules, and protocols that prevented the teaching of such an approach. I was heartbroken to hear this. Nonetheless, we continued to converse, and as our conversation drew to a close, he recommended that I explore the field of osteopathic medicine, which, at that time, had a reputation for being more holistic. I left his office at the end of the day feeling disheartened.

As fate would have it, later that week, I found myself shadowing the second doctor. Much to my surprise, she too asked me about my motivation for becoming a doctor. Brimming with enthusiasm, I gave her the same answer I had given the previous doctor. However, my excitement quickly transformed into disappointment when she also suggested that I explore osteopathic medicine. Researching osteopathy, I discovered that similar rules, regulations, and protocols apply, and I found myself grappling with uncertainty about how to reconcile my desire to teach people about the power of self-healing with the constraints of traditional medical practice.

Now what?

I felt lost.

This was something I always wanted to do.

The shattering realization that my ambition of becoming a doctor to teach others about self-healing may not be possible left me feeling uncertain about my future.

However, unwilling to allow my dreams to be completely dashed, I made a decision to take a break from my academic pursuits after graduation. I aimed to work in the medical field for the next two years as I figured out what my next steps would be.

I called upon the divine and my guides, seeking their guidance to help me determine my next steps.

One day, I was exploring different meetup events in my community to expand my social circle and happened upon a meditation group. As fate would have it, that's where I met a shaman woman who later became my spiritual guide and mentor.

It was remarkable to see how her classes evoked a sense of profound transformation within me. Through her teachings, I learned that I was a healer and even got the chance to connect with the lineage of medicine women in my family. I found myself visiting past lives where I was a medicine woman myself - an experience that was both enlightening and empowering.

Fascinated by my experiences with my spiritual teacher, I decided to sign up for her soul path package, which consisted of several one-on-one sessions aimed at unraveling the mysteries behind my purpose in life. One of these sessions involved a past life regression where my guide and I delved into what I was meant to do. During the regression, I witnessed a lineage of medicine women, including my previous life self, utilizing the earth's plants to heal their community and loved ones. As I reflected on this vision, I realized that utilizing the power of herbs to facilitate healing came to me naturally, almost like second nature. My spiritual guide recommended that I look into herbal medicine programs to see where this path might take me - and I did just that.

Intrigued by the idea of pursuing a career in herbal medicine, I decided to look up different programs that focused on this field. One particular school caught my eye, and it happened to be located close to where I lived. Excited, I wasted no time in checking out the school's website, and filled out and submitted an application. The following week, I was invited for an interview, and to my delight, was admitted on the spot into the master's program in acupuncture and traditional Chinese medicine.

I felt a rush of excitement and relief that maybe this holistic approach to medicine was the path I was supposed to take. Everything seemed to fall into place for me to get accepted into the program, and I felt eager to see where it would take me. And so, my journey to becoming an acupuncturist and herbal medicine practitioner began. This time, with an intense sense of enthusiasm and curiosity driving me, I could envision myself as an acupuncturist, already imagining what my future practice would look like.

This was it, right?

Coincidentally, while embarking on my journey to becoming an acupuncturist, I had the privilege of meeting my second spiritual guide and mentor. I devoted myself to a three-year program, aimed at delving deeper into my spiritual path. In this rigorous course of study, I joined a mystery school, which felt similar to receiving a doctoral level of spiritual schooling. A mystery school is an institution that teaches occult subjects such as Kabbalah, spiritual alchemy, shamanism, the high priestess path, ritual mastery, and more.

What struck me the most about acupuncture was how seamlessly it bridged the worlds of energetic practices and the more traditional medical knowledge that I gained during my pre-med education. The merge of the two was both beautiful and fascinating, and I quickly fell in love with this holistic form of medicine. Throughout my studies, I learned about the various meridians and channels of the human body, discovering ways to bring about harmony, balance, and healing through massage, acupressure, and the strategic insertion of acupuncture needles. It was an amazing experience.

My journey through the mystery school was extraordinary. It was here where I received several initiations that helped me evolve into a true spiritual alchemist, shaman, high priestess, ritual master, Kaballist, and ultimately, a healer and teacher. I deepened my meditations, learned how to sever negative energetic cords, and mastered the art of channeling high-frequency healing energies and messages. Connecting with my spiritual lineages became second nature, and I learned how to anchor my light into my body and the earth.

And that was just the beginning! I discovered how to work with my spiritual allies and family, learning how to harness their energies to achieve my dreams, goals and desires. My studies delved deeper into the spiritual nature of the body itself, and I learned about the power of ritual practices to support me in my spiritual path. The lessons I gained were endless and transformative.

I shared some of the spiritual tools I had picked up from the mystery school with my acupuncture classmates. They were curious to learn more, and would often approach me with questions such as: "How do you protect yourself from unwanted energies?", "How can I connect with my higher self?", "How can I connect with my animal guides?", "What are some ways to meditate effectively?", and "How can I release and heal the past?".

It felt rewarding to be able to offer my insight and knowledge to others, and I began to realize how interconnected these different aspects of my life truly were.

My classmates were so enthusiastic about learning from me that they requested I hold meditation classes for them. Excited to offer my skills and teachings, I happily agreed, and soon enough, the school discovered what I was doing and decided to open it up to the entire student body. Eventually, word of mouth spread, and the community expressed interest in my meditation classes as well.

In these classes, I taught my students various tools to help nourish and protect their energies, how to connect to their higher selves, cultivate relationships with spirit animals, angels and guides, and how to heal themselves while fine-tuning and balancing their energetic bodies. Along the way, I showed them how to channel divine healing energies to support their patients and so much more. It was a journey of exploration, spiritual growth, and healing for everyone involved.

During my final year of the program, I had the honor of being taken under the wing of one of my favorite teachers. He became my mentor, and introduced me to the world of esoteric acupuncture- a form of acupuncture that focuses on clearing and balancing the energy points in the body (Chakras) using sacred geometric patterns and a sequence of needle placement.

It's something he refused to teach to other students. When I asked him why he made this decision, he simply replied that he believed I was different; that I understood things that others couldn't quite grasp. And that's why he felt comfortable teaching me this advanced practice.

During one particular shadowing session, I mustered up the courage to ask my mentor a burning question that had been weighing heavily on my mind: "Do you see me as an acupuncturist?"

His answer was an unequivocal "No." I was shocked.

Sensing my confusion, he went on to elaborate, "Your work in this world is much bigger than this. While acupuncture certainly plays a role in your purpose, it is not the end goal for you. But don't worry – you will find your way."

His words served to both humble me and ignite a spark of curiosity within me. I knew that while I may not have all the answers yet, I had a special calling that was meant to be explored further.

And I couldn't say I was truly surprised by my mentor's response. I had already begun to sense that becoming an acupuncturist wasn't my ultimate destiny. In fact, a series of experiences had led me to question whether there was more to my calling than just this one specific profession.

One of these defining moments happened when I helped a client overcome a difficult challenge. She turned to me and said, "You know you could charge for this. People would be willing to pay you for your help." At the time, I brushed it off as a kind comment, but it planted a seed of curiosity within me.

As I continued to offer my classmates and fellow students a range of spiritual services and support, I began to realize that my gifts in this area were much more than a mere hobby or interest. Spirituality was my world; it came more naturally to me than anything else in this physical reality. I realized that this was my "genius zone," and there was so much more I could offer to those in need.

And whilst practicing acupuncture, I also noticed a curious phenomenon. Every time I placed a needle in someone, I could feel the energy flow through me and into their body. In fact, I didn't even need the needles to channel this energy - it seemed to come naturally to me.

Over time, my patients began to notice this too; they would schedule appointments exclusively with me because of the transformative healing they experienced during our sessions. Many of them told me that they could feel the energy flowing into them even before I placed the needle. And the effects of this healing energy were truly astonishing - they experienced profound shifts in their relationships, business, finances, and many other areas of their lives.

It was as if the healing energy they received during our sessions overflowed into all areas of their lives, bringing about positive change and transformation. It was clear to me that there was something special I was able to tap into, and it was my true calling in life to share it with others.

At the time, it felt like another journey that was meant for me had come to an end, and I felt crushed and disappointed. I had put so much time and energy into pursuing acupuncture, and now, it seemed like it might not be what I was meant to do.

I graduated with my master's of science in Acupuncture and traditional Chinese medicine. I was so proud of myself and who I had become through this enlightened journey. I came to realize that this journey had actually helped me step more fully into my purpose than I ever could have imagined. Despite not becoming an acupuncturist in the traditional sense, I had still gained a wealth of knowledge and skills that would serve me well in my future work.

In fact, I had discovered an entirely new way of healing - one that was more aligned with my gifts and calling than acupuncture ever could have been. I knew then that this was all part of the journey, and that everything that had happened so far was leading me towards my true life's work.

Following the completion of my studies, I rented an office space from an acupuncturist who had experienced the transformative power of my spiritual work firsthand. From this space, I continued to offer my services and began to expand my offerings even further.

Clients began coming to me for energy healing, activations, past life and future self-regressions, coaching, and much more. Over time, my reputation as a skilled and compassionate healer grew, and I was able to bring my unique gifts to an ever-increasing number of individuals.

Throughout it all, I continued to teach meditation classes, helping others to connect with their inner selves and discover the healing power of mindfulness practices. It was clear to me that the lessons I had learned through my studies and experiences, even those that didn't ultimately lead me down the path of acupuncture, had prepared me to make a real and meaningful difference in the lives of others.

As I continued my spiritual work with clients, I discovered a deep joy in walking people along their unique spiritual paths. There was something truly gratifying about helping someone connect with their true self and guiding them towards deeper healing and fulfillment.

What really set me apart from other practitioners, I realized, was my broad background in psychology, eastern and western medicine. It gave me a unique ability to anchor spiritual energies, which in turn led to quick manifestations and miraculous transformations.

Through my work, I was able to bridge the spiritual and the physical - the realm of heaven and the realm of earth - and help my clients understand their bodies and emotions in a way that simply wasn't taught in traditional schools. I could pinpoint exactly where in the body an imbalance lay, what emotions were tied to it, and even trace the roots of the trauma that caused it.

This holistic approach allowed us to dive deep and uproot the underlying issues that prevented my clients from experiencing true healing and growth. They began to see real, tangible results, and it was clear to me that this was my life's work - to empower and uplift others through my unique blend of spiritual, psychological, and medical expertise.

Today, I am proud to be the founder of Moon Goddess Academy and Publishing, an organization that exists to empower heart-centered women with the spiritual guidance and tools they need to awaken their sacred power and align with their true purpose.

As a Spiritual Guide, Mentor, Goddess Activator, Master Multidimensional Healer, Intuitive Channel, Seer, Oracle, and podcast host, I help women rediscover their why and reconnect with their true selves. I use my extensive knowledge and experience to provide mentorship, support, and spiritual guidance that allows women to tap into their inner strength and power, aligning themselves with their true purpose.

Through my work, I have helped countless women to create positive change in their lives, reminding them of their inherent power and supporting them as they unleash their full potential. I am committed to empowering women with the knowledge, tools, and guidance they need to live a life that is aligned with their true selves and values.

One of the most important takeaways from this chapter is that life rarely takes us on a straight path - and that's okay! Our purpose and calling in life often unfolds in unexpected ways, and we may not even realize the full extent of our journey until we're living it.

The soul journey is a process of discovery, and we learn and grow as we live our lives. It's important to embrace the twists and turns of our life path, even when they don't make sense at first. For it is through these experiences that we learn some of our most valuable lessons and often find our greatest strengths and passions.

So if you're feeling lost or unsure about your path in life, trust that there is a greater purpose at work. Keep an open mind, stay present in the moment, and allow yourself to discover the beauty and magic that is all around you. Who knows where your journey will take you? The only way to find out is to keep walking!

No matter where you find yourself on your journey, know that you are still on your soul's path. Trust the process and trust yourself, for the twists and turns of life can often lead us to unexpected and beautiful places.

It's important to remember that being human means finding our way and figuring things out as we go along. With each step forward, we gain greater clarity and insight into our purpose, passions, and how we can best serve the world around us.

While we may be tempted to compare our journey to others, remember that each path is different and unique. Honor your own journey and keep taking steps forward, for clarity will come with time and perseverance.

Even when our path seems to take us away from what we thought was our calling, trust that we are being led towards what truly resonates with our soul. Keep an open heart and an open mind, and allow yourself to embrace the wonder and joy of the journey, no matter where it takes you.

ABOUT THE AUTHOR

ABIGAIL MENSAH-BONSU

Abigail Mensah-Bonsu is a true powerhouse and visionary leader. As the founder of Moon Goddess Academy and Moon Goddess Publisher, she has built an empire of inspiration and empowerment that touches the lives of women across the globe. As a Spiritual Guide and Mentor, Goddess Activator, Master Healer, Intuitive Channel, Seer, Oracle, and International Bestselling Author, Abigail is a force to be reckoned with in the world of conscious impact.

Her passion and purpose are centered around helping influential women who may feel lost, disconnected, or unfulfilled. With her guidance and support, Abigail empowers these women to tap into their inner strength and align with their true purpose, creating a ripple effect of positive change that extends far beyond their own lives.

Abigail's life-changing work has been featured in prestigious publications such as Thrive Global and Life Grid magazine, and she has been a featured guest on countless podcast interviews and summits. Whether she's teaching spiritual tools to protect, amplify, and align with the sacred power within us all or helping women to rediscover their why and reconnect with their true selves, Abigail is a true master of her craft.

In her Colorado home with her loving husband and son, she delights in the simple pleasures of life, such as delicious teas, journals, pens, and markers. But make no mistake - when it comes to transforming lives and creating conscious impact, Abigail Mensah-Bonsu is a true force to be reckoned with, and her clients know that they're in the hands of a true visionary leader.

Connect with Abigail: https://linktr.ee/shaktimoongoddess
Grab your freebie, A meditation to help you find your center in the midst of the storms of life: https://www.moongoddessacademy.com/

2
ANGIE ATES-CLARK

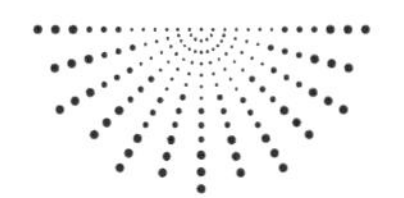

LIFE IS LIKE A WALK IN THE PARK

Some days you're strolling along the path with ease, and other days, you jump off the swings and scrape your knees.

Let me start by telling you this is not my story of 'rags to riches,' 'underdog to top dog,' or 'defeated to triumph,' though I have plenty to speak on about this. Instead, I intend to encourage you to 'walk in the park' with empowerment in the seasons of your life.

What I know is:

I am you.

I have never 'belonged.' My internal light shines bright and illuminates stuff in others. My raw intensity is only sometimes accepted or favored for relationship building or being included in activities. I have learned to recognize what is mine and what is not. I have learned to understand my gifts and all that comes with them..

What I know is:

My family has disowned me because I am 'different.'

I am not invited to family functions. I am gossiped about because of my 'natural' lifestyle and many other 'things.'

My father has repeatedly abandoned me and can only offer conditional love. He even told me he had wanted me aborted once, but my mom refused! I am here!

My ex-spouse of over 20 years had various extramarital affairs, including one with my close friend. He drained financial accounts and refused to support his children.

I have been on welfare. I have lived in my parent's basement with my kids to have a roof over our heads.

I have worked so much to ensure my kids were cared for that I have slept on my desk.

I had to pull over and sleep in my car because I could go no further.

I have been lied about.

I have been driven out of my hometown due to fear and vengeance. I have been exploited by those I trusted.

I have been stalked and death threats received. My tires have been flattened, and my house egged.

I have been denied promotions because I wouldn't sleep with upper management.

I have had bank accounts drained by those who 'loved' me.

I have had the church and Christians exploit, use, defame, and steal from me.

I have reached out to help people only to encounter Jezebels, who burned me at the cross.

I have shared my truth only to have it used against me.

I have had business partners who steal, lie, and manipulate the truth.

I have had incurable medical diagnoses. I healed them naturally.

I have worked my ass off, and I have had my ass handed to me.

I am you.

> ***"There are two types of pain in this world: pain that hurts you and pain that changes you!"* – Unknown**

The Walk in the Park

Walk with me as we stroll down the nature-filled path of the park. It is early morning; the sun has just started peeking through trees to shine warmth upon the path. We see squirrels playing, birds singing, and nature come to life.

We breathe in the fresh air, knowing we are breathing in life. This experience helps ground us and bring calm to our bodies. These are the times we are in balance. Our souls feel it. Our bodies bathe in the calm and glorious energy of nature. Our minds find peace on this path.

The park shows us the seasons of life. In the fall, we see the leaves die and celebrate a season well done in the cool crisp air of change. In the winter, we see the park come almost to a standstill as the elements go within, taking a rest for the season. We know the dormancy releases in the spring, and the colors return to the park, showing us that life is here again. In the summer, we hear kids' laughter, the sun's blazing energy rejuvenating all we do.

The park seasons reflect our seasons. When we step back and realize all relationships, careers, and situations have seasons, we are better equipped to prevail in the seasonal changes.

"For everything, there is a season and a time for every matter under heaven." **- Ecclesiastes 3:1-8**

The Teeter Totter

We look off to the right, and there is a teeter-totter seesaw. We walk over to it, reminiscing about when we were younger and enjoyed this park staple. The teeter-totter is fun as you go up and down with a velocity that depends on your totter partner. As you fly into the air, the joy comes out in laughter and freedom. Or maybe you are holding on tight because your totter partner is determined to throw you off. Do you see it? Do you feel it?

Now let's relate this teeter-totter experience to our real life. We all go through the ups and downs. Our partners contributing to this season may extract the joyful laughter with actions, words, and celebration of us. The totter experience takes place every second of the day. As we navigate the 'walk in the park' with careers, intimate partners, and various relationships, we must reposition ourselves to stay on the teeter-totter.

We also know that the totter experience can demand the need to hold on tight for dear life. Those moments when the other person is actively trying to throw you off the teeter-totter bring anguish, doubt, shame, and guilt, among other emotions, to the forefront. This situation may result in divorce, employment changes, and severed relationships involving gossip and lies.

This experience is when you can choose how long you want to stay holding on to that seat of the totter. Do you decide the experience is no longer aligned, so establish healthy boundaries and declare the need to be done? Do you continue to 'try harder' and keep holding on, expecting someone else to change or meet your needs?

This is where we are asked to reflect on the challenging teeter-totter experience and determine what part is our contribution and what part is our lesson. We tend to walk away with hurt feelings, raging emotional triggers, and loss on many levels.

We repeat experiences until healing occurs in our ancestral lineage. If you find a repeat of situations, I encourage you to find support in working on generational groups or past life aspects.

I work with people daily in these realms, assisting a root cause core resolution of healing. Contact me, and let's heal this together.

"Don't let others decide who you are." **- Denis Rodman**

The Dog Poop

I invite you to continue to take a 'walk in the park.' We enjoy our walk, breathing in the fresh air and experiencing the teeter-totter. We notice the fresh green grass and imagine our bare feet touching the soft new blades. We remove our shoes and stand there in the warmth of the grass and the sun shining on our faces. This grounding, this connection to the earth, this pause to soak up the experience is what the soul craves.

We find that we don't slow down enough anymore. We rush to this and that, frequently in the fight-flight-freeze mode. Although we know this constant race through time creates stress upon our minds and ultimately manifests as dis-ease in the body, we seem to be mesmerized by the expectations tied to our worth. Many times, it is the 'do' versus the 'be' that is rewarded.

Standing in the grass soaking up this experience brings us back to the reality of our choices—the truth of what we are doing in our lives. In reality, while connecting to mother earth, I encourage you to breathe, pause, and reset. Repeat this moment anytime you need to re-align to your heart's center- your soul's work.

Now that you have paused to appreciate all that God has provided us for healing this pain of 'not enough,' I ask you to continue to walk with me barefoot through the luscious green grass.

Just ahead, you will find a beautiful swaying willow tree. Let's walk over to it as it represents so much. It's a symbol of fertility and new life; a willow branch can be planted in the ground, and a new tree will grow in its place. Its ability to grow and survive is powerfully symbolic and shows how we can thrive even in challenging conditions.

You stroll through the lush green grass and begin to soak up the magnificent aspects of the willow tree. You recognize that this symbolizes your strength in all aspects of your life.

You are almost to the tree. It is in your sight. You see its magnificence. And on this last step..hmmm. Something under your foot does not seem to belong on this peaceful stroll . It is dog poop!

That's right. Just as you have your clarity, focus, purpose, and goals, in comes 'shit.'

This may present as:

Bull shit - not true

Horseshit - nonsense

Apeshit - rambunctious

Batshit - insane

Chickenshit - coward

Ratshit- poor quality

No shit- obviously

Holy shit - mind blowing / unbelievable

Hot shit - very good

Dipshit - a total dumbass

Tough shit - take it or leave it

Jack shit - nothing

The Shit - perfection

Many times this 'shit' isn't even yours. You stepped into it, not knowing it was there. You inherit the 'shit,' and now you must clean it up. Or someone brings the 'shit' and dumps on you to take care of. Either way, your response is your choice, albeit often triggered by something more profound.

When the 'shit' hits the fan, emotional triggers will occur. You may even begin to doubt your abilities or believe other people's thoughts about the situation.

You get to choose your response to the 'shit.' You also get the opportunity to dig deep and heal the 'shit.'

This healing takes place in many forms. My favorite is to get to the root cause of all the 'shit' and begin situation by situation to heal, transform, remove, and seal it. I love to hear from my clients as they feel the difference in our work together and experience the healing in real time as situations arise.

Because you are equipped and empowered to be ready for moments like this, you reach into your bag and locate a thick wet wipe to remove the 'shit' that now has immersed your big toe.

You recognize and honor your growth as, this time; you were ready. There was no 'drama.' There was no 'chaos.' You prepared with ease and grace to confront and heal all the 'shit.' You, my friend, are brilliant! You, my friend, are worthy of so many blessings. It is time to CTSO - clear the shit out.

I am your biggest fan. I love seeing your success through your eyes of reality.

And you know WHY?

Because *I am you.*

Now that you have removed the 'shit,' let's continue to that willow tree. It is swaying back and forth and ready for you to shelter under its long exquisite branches. You may stop for a reprieve, a reset, or to fill yourself up with love.

The value is in the pause! This pause is powerful as you allow yourself to breathe and reflect on life as you are experiencing it. Carving out those moments that allow you to reset and remember will equip you for life and empower you to stand in your genius with clarity.

> ***"You've got enemies? Good, that means you stood up for something in your life."*** **– Eminem**

The Mud Puddles

As we continue our 'walk in the park,' we start to feel raindrops. We feel the air shift and a clean smell surrounds us. We make our way over to a covered park bench, where we wait out the raindrops. As we take a reprieve from the rain, we laugh and realize that, once again, mother nature is cleansing our thoughts and clearing our energetic fields. In these fields, we collect other people's energy that weighs us down. We sit smiling and reflecting on our life before the rain.

We know that what follows good rain are mud puddles. When the puddles begin to form, our thoughts go back to when we were young. We would jump in the puddles with such happiness and laughter. Oh, that laughter again! Our parents would tell us not to hit that puddle: "You have your good shoes on." We, of course, would jump anyway.

Bring the mud puddle full circle right now as you sit on the bench, watching it fill up with rainwater. We have many choices when the puddle in our life begins to form. We can ignore it and pray it goes away. We can take quick action to ensure we walk around the mud puddle. We can just jump in the puddle, enjoying the splash, the moment, and the clearing of the muddy water. The choice is always ours.

Storms, rain, and even mud puddles provide us with many gifts. The gift of a storm is to recognize what really matters in our lives. We tend to 'hustle' even when it is not required.

Society has ingrained in us to 'do more,' 'be more,' and 'own more.' The storm, whether a death, a divorce, a job change, or something else significant in our life, brings us back to reality. The storm is scary but worth it as it moves through, and the sun begins to shine her warmth again on our lives. Clarity is presented, and a choice to maintain the post-storm experience is offered.

The rain, albeit frustrating at times, waters all life. The rain rinses the grime, feeds the plants, and ensures a healthy life cycle. The rain knows no boundaries, only the boundaries or containers we channel it to. The rain can symbolize so many aspects of our life.

The mud puddles are waiting to hear your laughter! The mud puddles remind us to play like a child. To stomp in that puddle with dry, new shoes laughing the entire time. Take the time. Do it for you. Laugh a lot and dance in the rain.

> ***"Life isn't about waiting for the storm to pass but learning to dance in the rain."*** **- Vivian Greene**

The Sunset Walk

Our day has been filled with adventure. We enjoyed our 'walk in the park' today. We embraced the swings as high as we could go. We have been slung off the merry-go-round because we could not hold on any longer. We enjoyed the teeter-totter flying high while our partner laughed with us. We have even taken up a yard game of croquet.

You were so proud of yourself as you used your mallet and hit that ball right through the hoops. While you did not make it every time, you let your inner child laugh and have fun.

As we walk down that same beautiful nature-filled path we started with, we notice the sun is setting. The cotton candy skies with the final warm glow from the sun bouncing off everything. We acknowledge all we have done today, celebrate our wins, and appreciate the lessons.

The sun setting is a season that can be woven into so many experiences. Maybe you are not where you expected to be in life.

After all, you did all the right things. You took the courses. You did the energy work. You have helped others and given to many. You have completed leadership programs to communicate better. You have hired coaches and mentors to help you along the way. But still, you feel like the sun is setting and there will be no tomorrow.

What I know is:

I am you.

I challenge you to look deep inside yourself. The 'walk in the park' we take is challenging. We can shift our mindset. We can think positively. All of these qualities and developed skills help during these seasons.

However, I have found that when you dig underneath the conscious mind and find the wiring that really guides us, we can heal to a whole new level.

Here I will tell you about my experience. It was not until I had many past lives healed and transformed and many generational aspects healed and restored did I find PEACE. I, too, did all the work. I, too, did all the right things. But during these outside-the-box methods, I discovered a healing that words can not explain. During these experiences, my cellular memory and the messages I sent to the world were different!

I went on to get the training to expand my gifts to the world. As an alternative practitioner, traditional naturopath, and full mesa shaman, I could blend all this knowledge and partner it with medical intuitive training to help many.

If you are struggling and have done 'all the things,' I encourage you to step out in faith and align with a trained professional to guide you along this 'walk in the park.'

We all deserve to shine our genius upon the world with ease and grace.

"The secret to life is meaningless unless you discover it yourself."
- W. Somerset Maugham

ABOUT THE AUTHOR

ANGIE ATES-CLARK

Angie Ates-Clark is a leading Intuitive Business Strategist who works with female entrepreneurs helping them create a conscious ethos as a feminine leader.

She's spent over 3 decades equipping, empowering and training over 10,000 professionals globally. She's a multiple #1 international bestselling author and recognized speaker.

She spent over 20 years in Corporate Executive Leadership, where she was known for her talent scouting and succession planning strategies.

After multiple autoimmune diagnoses she repurposed her life; educating herself on integrative healthcare solutions including energy medicine. Ultimately launching successful 6-figure health clinics, which served over 5000 clients.

She's been featured in over 250 training videos, multiple summits and served as a co-host of several podcasts.

Whether she's sharing stages with Les Brown or facilitating a Corporate Wellness Program she's regularly 'shaking up the status quo' to inspire people to take action quickly, helping them achieve unprecedented results.

You'll find her traveling the world with her husband Don, or spending time with her 3 children - her inspiration for life.

Contact: office@AngieAtes.com

573.204.1111 office #

FB: https://www.facebook.com/DrAngieAtes

www.AngieAtesClark.com

3

ELIZABETH FORBES-STOBBE

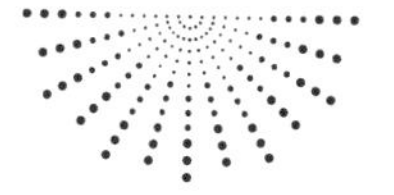

MY KALEIDOSCOPIC MIND

Ever peeped into a kaleidoscope?

It's a wholesome experience.

At one glance, you'll see multi-coloured balls running around in myriad directions. There is so much clutter that it's impossible to decipher the pattern amidst the madness. The sheer activity of looking through the kaleidoscope can be meditative as it allows you to focalize your vision and concentrate your energies on the different designs and configurations which are formed due to the reflection of multiple mirrors. Only when you stay patient and focussed, can you see the balls arranging themselves in magnificent patterns.

Just as a flicker of light has the power to pierce the darkness, getting the right direction amidst chaos can enable an individual to navigate through uncertainty and touch great heights.

Being Invisible

My younger self was brimming with unbridled creativity, however I lacked an effective outlet to channel my energy and attain my true potential.

My childhood years in Trinidad are characterized by immense joy and hyperactivity. My head was like a kaleidoscope, filled with myriads of ideas, thoughts and perspective.

I was constantly grappling with a myriad of ruminations and speculations, which made me a day-dreamer. To make sense of my mind-boggling thoughts, I would often doodle or paint as it soothed my heart and soul, but it did not amount to anything significant as far as academic success was concerned.

My performance was evaluated solely by the marks I scored, not by my contribution in class or my creative inputs during discussions and debates. My head was in the clouds so I could rarely pay attention to the task at hand. At that time, no one had an inkling of my medical condition as I was experiencing the symptoms of ADHD (Attention Deficit Hyperactivity Disorder) which was identified at a later stage of my life.

My teacher felt that I was distracted so I was often perceived as an "undisciplined girl" who could achieve extraordinary milestones if she inculcated the art of immersing herself in deep work. My parents were strict and unbending as they also believed that I lacked the grit and determination to become the ideal child whom they could take pride in. They mistook my innate curiosity for obstinacy which further pressured me to numb my distinct creative streak and mould myself into the typical child who was obedient and submissive. Their towering expectations became a prison for me as I was compelled to suppress the dynamic aspects of my personality.

Slowly, I was rendered invisible as I became a version of myself that was more of a badge of honour for them. I was like a wired doll who was a cumulation of parental and social expectations. As a coping mechanism, I took to reading which was therapeutic. I inhabited the world of my imagination when I flipped through the pages of my book. There, I could be anyone I wanted to be. There were no rigid pre-defined molds to curb my self-expression.

Gradually, reading became a window to my escape and my bedroom was my safe haven. I identified with strong and bold female protagonists who took the reins of their life in their own hands and carved their legacy. The love for stories was deepened by my aunt who used to narrate fascinating stories in her distinct animated style. When she weaved magic through her voice and words and presented enchanting scenarios, I became so engrossed that I would forget all my apprehensions and challenges.

In the eyes of my loved ones, I was an "average child" who was just good enough compared to her talented sibling.. I also aspired to be worthy, unique and independent, just like them, . but as I struggled to fit in, I drifted away from my authentic self.

During the moments of doubt and despair, I would often derive immense comfort and inspiration from a captivating butterfly. I saw them when I used to play with my grandfather in the fields.

When I observed the butterfly, I used to marvel at how free and fearless it was. Its vibrant wings would add a dash of magic and colour to my monochromatic life. I wanted to be just like the butterfly, full of life and vigour, liberated.

As I had to subdue my creativity, it created a clash between the disparate selves. The constant tussle between my obedient and curious selves bothered me tremendously, creating havoc within my head. It would take over 30 years before I was able to declutter my mind by navigating through the disorder and choosing who I wanted to be — by claiming my path and rewriting my destiny.

Originality and authenticity are treasured gifts which make us who we are. People around us might strive hard to take our individuality away from us by pressuring us to follow the herd but we should stay true to our dreams and goals. It is only when we listen to our inner compass that we can achieve extraordinary milestones both professionally and personally.

Embracing the Unknown, Rising through the Challenges

The entrepreneurial streak runs in the family as my grandfather was a shoe-maker. He was a part of the cottage industry and made world-class shoes by hand. I had a deep connection with him as he always encouraged me to become the best version of myself. He taught me to tap into my inner reserves of strength and talents and strive for brilliance. Over time I would realize my true potential and fulfill my dreams.

When I completed my education, I began my professional journey as a post office clerk, but it didn't appeal to my sensibilities. I wanted to pursue a career path where I could exercise my creative talents and compassionate nature more profoundly. Gradually, I made a career pivot and became a teacher for kindergarten children. While I thoroughly enjoyed nurturing the kids, I deepened my drive to make a significant impact on my community by looking after people, especially the elderly.

Eventually, my life took an interesting turn when I was called for nurse training in the UK. After successfully completing my training, I worked in an NHS hospital as a nurse and ward manager. It was an incredibly illuminating experience for me as I was entrusted with the responsibility of running a ward. I was performing a hands–on role which included managing staff teams, training and teaching new recruits. The responsibility was grave as people's lives were in our hands, so I inculcated the crucial skills of meticulous planning and people management, whilst honing my social and interpersonal skills.

While I was navigating through the challenges of work, my struggles intensified as I was constantly battling with innumerable distractions internally. There were episodes of failure and setbacks which reminded me of the "distracted girl" label which I was actively trying to let go of..

As someone who was experiencing ADHD, it was tough to manage the chaos of my mind. Many times, I had to mask the hyperactivity of my mind as it would often go out of control. It was tough to manage the dynamic interplay of thoughts but I had learned the technique of listening to sounds around me to prevent intense distractions. Initially, my outbursts used to manifest themselves as unwanted gestures like tapping the table during serious staff meetings. However, I trained my mind to discipline my thoughts so that I could fare well in those challenging scenarios.

To approach it more systematically, I followed actionable strategies like breaking up complex tasks into small items to understand and execute them better, maintaining a to-do list to ensure that all the processes are performed to the T and setting a timer for duties which had a strict deadline. Along with achieving productivity at work, I also prioritised my self-care by taking regular breaks and following a healthy lifestyle. With every passing day, I was excelling in my line of profession and was slowly reaching closer to my calling.

As I was thriving on my professional front, a refreshing chapter began as romance knocked on my door when I met the man who would become my husband.. There was an instant connection as I felt that I had met my match intellectually. He understood me deeply and made me feel alive. We were compatible in terms of ideologies and worldviews. Eventually, we got married as he was "the one" for me. I could not wait to step into my happily ever after with him.

But things altered for us dramatically once we got married. As circumstances changed, our chemistry began to fade as our priorities shifted. Slowly, he began to undermine me and took every opportunity to dominate over me. This shattered my self-esteem as I began to question my worth. Even though a lot of rebellion was emerging within me, I chose to remain silent to make the relationship work. I did not want to live with the baggage of a failed marriage so I decided to endure every ounce of humiliation that I felt, hoping against hope that one day, he would realize his flaws and then, he would keep his ego aside and work to bridge the distance which was emanating within us.

But silence is not always helpful to mend bridges. Sometimes, it is your worst enemy as it projects a docile and submissive side of your personality for people to take advantage of. The tipping point for me came when I could no longer tolerate the negativity he brought in my life.

I felt stifled by the criticism so I doubled my efforts to solidify my career and created a world for myself within the space of my work. I was very proud of the car I had bought but his insecurity was so intense that he took it away and gave me a new one. He took a piece of my individuality and coloured me like he wanted me to be. This episode left an indelible impact in my life, making me realize that I no longer wanted to be his shadow. I wanted to build something of my own to echo my values and beliefs.

Grapes have to undergo tremendous pressure to transform into wine, which is considered to be its finest form. We gain enormous resilience through adversity. It is only when we are daring enough to step into the chaos, we are able to survive and evolve.

Fit for Purpose, Discovering my calling

I took a leap of faith and started my own health and social care business. As a general and psychiatric nurse, I started a group for people who had memory problems. My mission was to provide preventive treatment for elderly people.

My philosophy of caring and nurturing is infused with compassion and empathy. It is not a mechanical performance of a series of steps by reading through a medical guidebook. Rather, I believe in tending to every patient distinctly by understanding the nuances of their emotions and feelings.

Through my business, I wanted to provide the care which I believed in. Like I would do for my mother. Passion was my driving force as I was holding on the vestiges of faith to build something extraordinary.

When I started out, I didn't have a business plan but I knew that I wanted to serve my community. There was no structure in the business sense in the initial days but when the team expanded, the structure came in organically.

I taught myself by reading books like *Business for Dummies.* Gradually, the business took on a life of its own and I opened my wings to soar new heights.

On the professional front, I was thriving, on the personal front, my marriage was bringing me down. Finally, I made the call to file for divorce. While the divorce saved me from the control of my arrogant husband, it brought me to the lowest phase of my life. It was the most challenging step as it brought about a series of personal turmoil. My physical and mental health deteriorated as I was trying hard to cope with the grief and resentment. While I was seeing a therapist, I was informed about my ADHD and I decided to seek medical assistance to tackle it.

During my sessions with the counsellor, I got to know about the negative thought pattern which was affecting my self-perception. Moreover, I learned about the intricacies of attaining "flow state" which is integral in succeeding in our creative pursuits. Flow state refers to a sense of fluidity between our mind and body when we are deeply focused on something, beyond the point of distraction. In that span of time, our senses are heightened. It is as if time flies as we achieve effortless momentum with our actions.

With concerted efforts, I was able to reconcile with the disorganized thoughts and scattered perceptions to bring more mental clarity and emotional well-being.

Our mind is our most powerful asset as it is forever brimming with innovative thoughts and ideas. It is imperative that we learn to master our thoughts by practising discipline and focus. If you want your business to thrive, you must be willing to walk an extra mile to rise above mediocrity and attain excellence.

Choosing Fight over Flight: Not Sorry Anymore

As I was finding my way back by hurtling through the darkness, a ray of hope emerged in the form of a life-changing episode when I crossed paths with a toxic landlord who tried to oppress me, just like my husband.

Once I moved out of the marital house, I decided to rent a place for myself as I was seeking some peace and solitude. I paid a huge sum of money for one year but didn't realize it back then.

Even though I was overcoming the trauma and treading on the path of recovery, there were moments of intense vulnerability. I did not realize how brittle I was until that fateful day when I heard a loud banging on a door early in the morning.

I got scared at once but mustered some courage to see who it was. I was amazed to see that my landlord was standing outside, shouting where's the rent? I was dazed and didn't know how to approach this situation. But suddenly, something triggered within me and my pent up rage resurfaced.

A realization dawned upon me. I began to fathom how unfair the entire situation was. It took me back to those moments when aggressive men talked down to me, misconstruing my congeniality for my inner weakness. The landlord was questioning my integrity and implying that I had not paid the rent ? A dormant yet powerful voice within me spoke, "Liz, why are you allowing this man to talk to you like this? You don't deserve this. Speak up and take a stand for yourself."

I confronted him with all my might and shouted, "How dare you come to my house? Don't dare to speak to me like that again."

In that moment, I regained my determination and grit to fight and take a stand for myself. That was a breakthrough for me as I expressed my anger which resulted in a distinct kind of healing.There was no going back from that moment.

Having faith during tough circumstances can be life-changing. Without hope, you will forever be in despair. Getting up in the morning when you face adversity can be the bravest thing you can do. Courage is not always loud and roaring, sometimes it is subtle which helps us to power through difficulties.

Illuminating my World: Building my Candle Making Business

As COVID struck the world, it altered my life trajectory. I couldn't step out due to my Inflammatory bowel disease so I had to isolate myself. I was standing at the crossroads as I could not pursue my nursing business anymore.I found myself asking, "Who am I when I am not a nurse? What new dimension can I explore?"

My answer came through a flicker which illuminated my world, literally and metaphorically!

I have always loved luxury and scented candles. So I pursued my love for candle-making and got formal certification for the craft. I educated myself through videos and books to learn the nuances of this art. Moreover, I learned to create my own formulations, did intensive field research, got feedback from experts and honed my craft.

My goal was simple – I wanted to make my high-quality candles and sell them at an affordable price. Even though I was out of my comfort zone, it was immensely enriching and gratifying.

ADHD made my mind go to a thousand places. When I melted the wax, added the alluring fragrance, and poured it into my candle jars, I could process my thoughts and attain a meditative state where I explored my spiritual side. Moreover, it trained me to focus on the present moment and appreciate the blissful pleasures of life.

My favourite part was to savour the moments of accomplishments, admiring the magnificent candles I'd created after hours of continuous hard work and dedication.

My entrepreneurial side evolved. I mastered the technique of candle making which involved testing the oil, learning about the temperature and working with the wick. I also arranged for equipment like diffusers which were integral in making beautiful candles. My kitchen became my workshop where I mixed all the hand-made products which I created using the finest ingredients - my oils were from England and Scotland and for my wax, I used a mix of rapeseed and coconut oil to create luxurious candles.

My goal was to understand the technical dynamics of this art form. By creating meticulous notes and multiple rounds of trial and error,

I created my own unique formula which became a differentiating factor for my business. My candles were perfect for creating a cosy ambience and a fragrant mood to any room.

I intended to target the wellness industry and hoped to carve a niche for myself there. With time, I transformed my passion into my profession and created She Makes Candles 2.0.

Along with the creative aspect, I ventured out of my comfort zone to explore the financial aspect by getting insurance for my company. I also enlightened myself about the legal intricacies and testing regulation to ensure that everything was in place.

The philosophy behind my brand is to evoke charming memories and emotions through enticing fragrances. Making the luxury candles is a labour of love for me, a medium through which I attain peace of mind amidst disorder. Moreover, I wanted to carve a niche for myself.

One of the characters from whom I derive immense inspiration and comfort from is Po from the movie Kung Fu Panda. Bustling with energy, passion and enthusiasm, he had infinite potential to achieve wonders. And yet, he had to go through a journey of personal evolution to fulfil his dream of becoming the Kung Fu Master and save the Valley of Peace.

His transformation, under the guidance of the wise tortoise Master Oogway and his protégé, the red panda Master Shifu, shed light on some key lessons which every entrepreneur should keep in mind to attain success and make a significant impact.

Po takes a leap of faith and ventures into the unknown as he firmly believes in his dream. Although he was working in his father's noodle shop, he challenged his limitations to find his true calling. His action-oriented mindset, grit and resilience during his training period made him into a professional Kung Fu Master. But for me, the most encouraging insight was his ability to fight through distractions and discover his individuality.

In the words of Master Oogway, "Your mind is like this water, my friend. When it is agitated, it becomes difficult to see. But if you allow it to settle, the answer becomes clear."

Only when you are original in your ideas and approach, can you succeed in business.

Gradually, I was able to channel my aggression in the right direction and sublimate the negative emotions. The more I stayed with myself, the more introspective I became. With time, I embraced my anger and disrupted the walls of denial which I had built around myself to emerge free, in the true sense.

There is a lot of strength, humility and grace in trying and failing repeatedly. If you have taken the first step towards building your dream company, then you are on the path of limitless growth and wisdom. Never give up due to the fear of failure. Instead, adopt a growth mindset and turn every setback as a learning opportunity which can help you become better than yesterday.

Reinventing myself in my fifties

Today, I am tremendously appreciated for my products and my clients express their gratitude. My candles add a dash of magic to their special days. She Makes Candles 2.0 is not just the thriving startup, it is a medium through which I serve my community through my creativity.

Just like my nursing business, the candles I create are meant to spread positivity, hope and happiness. In the words of Tagore, "I slept and dreamt that life was joy. I awoke and saw that life was service. I acted and behold, service was joy."

Chaos is not just the mind, it is also those scattered emotions, those half-baked judgments that people made because they couldn't understand who I truly was. Only when I realized my true worth, when I fought for my self-respect, passions and purpose, did I discover that those disorganised elements were actually a stepping stone for me to realize my innate beauty. I no longer feel lost but empowered as I have found my voice and identity.

My mental kaleidoscope needed intense training and emotional awareness to decipher the method amidst the madness. The one thing I want you to know, is that beauty is not found in a flawless state, it is discovered amidst chaos and agitation. You just need to have the eye for it!

Struggles and difficulties can be painful, but they can often lead to growth and change. Eventually, we find novel ways to pivot and overcome hurdles effectively. We become stronger and more capable when we are forced to confront our limitations.

FIVE LIFE LESSONS WHICH I STAND BY EVEN TODAY

- Don't give up even when the going gets tough
- Know your strengths and tap into their potential
- Keep it simple and elegant
- Derive joy and inspiration from your work
- Trust your gut instinct and take pride in your uniqueness

ABOUT THE AUTHOR

ELIZABETH FORBES-STOBBE

Elizabeth Forbes-Stobbe is a nurse, award winning multipassionate entrepreneur , author and chandler. Her motto is to never give up, there is always a way to solve the problems. She loves working with people who know what they want to achieve. She sold her first healthcare business after 10 years and founded a home fragrance business in 2022 hand making candles and at the time of writing this book a home help service.

She has also written 2 books 'Lead with Care' and 'I AM'. Elizabeth has been featured in Health Care magazines, the Daily Mail, Essex Life magazine, the Voice Newspaper and Take a Break magazine.

She lives in the UK where she continues to illuminate her world by serving the community. Elizabeth loves dancing and dining out on her own.

You can find her on www.shemakescandles.com , www.beaulieucare.com

Instagram: elizabeth_forbesstobbe

Twitter: @ElizabethStobbe

4
EMMA STARLING

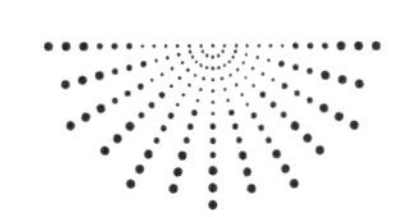

A NEW REALITY AT YOUR FINGERTIPS

"I'm out aren't I?" he said, as the air in the room crackled with tension.

You could hear a pin drop. My heart was beating loudly in my ears, but strangely steady.

"Yeah, you are. I'm sorry, but I can't keep choosing this as my reality."

The words slipped out of my mouth effortlessly, my voice calm and resolute. His response? Total shock and disbelief, followed by belligerence and denial. I knew at that moment that I had made the right decision. The decision that had evaded me for years, or rather, that I had actively avoided.

I took a deep breath and levelled my gaze, settling my eyes on his. I was ending a 12 year relationship. I was changing everything I had known for the bulk of my adult life. The decision had not come lightly to me, in fact I had been back and forth about it for a few years.

There was a ringing in my ears. Echoes of all the conversations I'd had with myself, and with him. Flashes of memories behind my eyes, faster than I could catch consciously. I reached for the granite worktop, cold and steady underneath my palm.

I made myself recount the reason I was doing this. There were lots of them and there was also one big one. I had reached the lowest point in our relationship and I knew I needed to keep that front of mind for the next few days as things unravelled around me.

I used the tools I had been teaching others for years already. I gently rubbed my collarbone and breathed slowly into the pit of my belly. To any onlooker I may have just looked nervous. In reality, I was stimulating the K27 point, an acupressure point that is incredibly soothing in times of stress or upset.

I slowly looked around me, and placed my attention on something that was pleasant to look at - my beautiful Rottweiler, Boss, lying on the kitchen rug, blissfully unaware anything was wrong. I took in everything about him, regulating my nervous system. My heart skipped a beat. I didn't care what I came away with in this uncoupling as long as my dog remained with me. That was a non negotiable. He had always been mine, that was not about to change. The rest was just stuff. As it happened, that belief served me well when I returned to my home a few days later to find the paltry remnants of the life we had built there.

As I set to redecorating and changing the furniture I felt a sense of liberation. I was finally free from the anxiety, the self-doubt and the rock bottom self-esteem that had plagued me for years. I had taken control of the situation and decided that I had absolutely had enough. It wasn't the first time I had been let down and it wouldn't be the last. I knew that, if I stayed any longer, I was literally choosing that for myself. In reality, I had been all along. From the very first deceit, right through to the final nail in the relationship coffin.

Part of me loathed myself for not leaving earlier. Part of me didn't want to cause him any pain. For every reason I had to leave, my ego mind gave me a reason it was my fault, or a way I could have kept trying. I had been trained to believe things were my fault. I was the deserter, and if I just looked a certain way or wore a certain pair of shoes, things would be ok. If only it were that simple. No matter how hard I tried, and I did for years, it was never enough. Learned helplessness kicked in because, well, what's the point, right?

There was no violence. Part of me would love to believe there was no malice either, only poor judgement. Either way, the impact on me had been catastrophic over the years. My house and decor was devoid of personality. Things I loved were confined to one room out of the way because it constituted clutter. No matter how hard I tried, I couldn't correctly fit into the mould that was just waiting for me to step into, so that everything could be perfect. I blamed myself for years.

Then, watching a soap opera on TV, where the storyline involved coercive control, I realised what had been going on and I felt sick to my stomach. In a split second, the decision was made.

This wasn't the first break up I had been through. It was the first one I had instigated however that didn't take me out at the knees. I had prepared for it. I had done the work. I had cried my tears. I had questioned myself. I had torn myself apart with guilt about it. I didn't want to hurt anybody. I just wanted to slip quietly out the door and start a new life, and that's pretty much what happened. At 8am the next morning me and my dog drove back to my parents' house, throwing the dice up in the air to fall however they may.

It wasn't the first time we had broken up either, although this time it was permanent. There was not one ounce of me that doubted it. As I sat at my parents' dining table, recounting the event, I stroked Boss's head and smiled. Everything I needed was in that room. I actually felt calm, safe and free. I knew we were going to be ok no matter what happened next as long as I honoured my decision.

It wasn't always like this. I had always struggled with anxiety and low self-esteem to one degree or another, from very early on. My earliest memory of it starting was when I was five or six years old, and was putting out hymn books in church. Somehow I did it wrong and everybody laughed at me. I never went back.

They're known as "hot stove moments", in that the shock to your system from the shame inducing event stays in your system unless dealt with. Over time they compound and, for a highly sensitive child, this can be low self-esteem inducing at best.

My journey through school was blighted by verbal bullying and feeling like an outsider. Between the ages of 11 and 31, I was systematically rejected and shamed by friends, boyfriends and authority figures. Two boyfriends even left me for "somebody better" and actually told me that!

The deputy head teacher at my senior school shamed and humiliated me in front of the entire class aged 14 by telling me that, with a backside and legs like mine, I shouldn't even wear trousers, let alone a skirt. Charming man whose humour cut me like a knife.

Imagine all the things you think are wrong with you. Then, one by one, they are confirmed as true by people you trust. If that doesn't rock your sense of self and make you feel not good enough, I don't know what would, but I didn't let anybody see.

I hid my feelings away like the crown jewels and instead went into extrovert overcompensation mode. Sarcasm, self-deprecation and starvation diets became the new modus operandi for me, at least for a while. My way of feeling safe and okay back then, was to take the power away from those who would hurt me.

If I was thin, they couldn't call me a fat bitch. If I was self-deprecating, they couldn't get to me first. If I was sarcastic, they wouldn't see that I was really hurting. That tactic saw me through nicely until I went to university, at which point I had to up my game.

I was living away from home this time. My ultimate safety net was no longer there. I took solace once again in food, but now also in money. The Next Directory did very well out of me between 1994 and 1998 and I'm pretty sure I owned one of everything they sold at one point. I found my groove in the 70s disco lights, the curve-hugging-but-not-slutty dresses and cute shoes, pulling people's eyes towards me while I danced the night away most Tuesdays, Fridays and Saturdays.

You could be forgiven even for thinking I was an extrovert at this point. I became a professional in the art of deflection. Little did I know at the time I was drifting further and further away from who I really was. I left university with a 2:2 in French and German that I chastised myself about for years. Within the decade that followed I lost my job and my house and my relationship on the same day, twice within a four year span. By this point, even my bank manager was calling me a tough little cookie.

I know loss and difficulty are things we all have to go through in this life. For a regulated human being who has a healthy sense of who they are, I would imagine this early part of my life would have been a lot easier. As for me, I stumbled from crutch to crutch looking outside of myself for safety, validation and the ensuing happiness I believed it would bring. I had no idea who I was. I was riddled with self-doubt and don't even get me started on the lack of boundaries and people-pleasing.

When your internal compass is shot, and your heart is in tatters, it's incredibly easy to lose yourself in the next bright shiny thing or promise of comfort, safety and connection. A narcissistic relationship was definitely not on my bucket list of things to do in my 30s and 40s. Yet somehow I had attracted one. The first few weeks I felt alive, sexy and seen. I'd never experienced that before and I was hooked. The adrenaline coursing through me like an electric current took over my rational decision-making abilities and crushed my desire for anything and everything else.

The web I was caught in was so strong that I overlooked red flags over and over again until around January 2020. At that time, I embarked on a certification that totally changed my life. I learned that my sense of self-worth was a result of a family paradigm that I had been given that had created rules and set points for how much I felt I deserved.

I was already trained in Emotional Freedom Technique (EFT), a tapping technique to balance your energy, but training as a Tapping Into Wealth Coach enabled me to uncover and dissolve the real roots of my lack of self-worth. Decades of patterning began to fall away immediately. The fog began to lift and I felt increasingly resilient.

By April, I had submitted my resignation letter to my employer of seven years, so I could go full-time with the business I'd been building up around it. By August, I was ready to leave the relationship in question.

By November, I sold my beloved house and moved back home to be closer to the family I'd been away from for so long. That moment is just as clear in my memory banks as the relationship breakup.

I'd been deliberating for a while over whether to stay in the house and maintain a big mortgage, or sell up. By this point, I was a lot clearer about who I was and what I wanted due to all the energy work I'd been doing. So I applied my tools. I got quiet and went inside for the answer.

What met me was an unshakable sense of self trust that I should go home, and I signed the paperwork to sell the house the very next day. Once again, that decision was a catalyst for massive change because those proceeds paid off the £50,000 of debt I'd amassed as an adult that stemmed from low self-esteem, low self-worth and trying to please people. Or maybe it was to buy their affections, I'm still not sure which. I use the term adult here very loosely because I really didn't feel like one most of the time.

The one thing that changed was the realisation that safety and security don't come from outside of us. They come from inside, always have done. When you learn how to dissolve the interconnecting layers of programmes and patterns we all carry, feeling safe becomes easy. When you get it right and identify the core worthiness wounds, the big hitters, you collapse the recovery time frame immeasurably.

When you feel safe within yourself, you trust yourself. When you trust yourself and you can surrender and receive all the good stuff that the Universe can bring you. When you surrender, you can make decisions and take action from a point of stillness, not stress and contraction. You connect back into your truth. When you surrender and connect back into yourself and your truth, you become unbreakable. That's the point where you are able to tolerate what I call "the contrast". You learn how to shift your entire reality.

That icky feeling you get that's part and parcel of carrying around a mixed bag of emotions? That's contrast. When you're adrift, the contrast can sink you. When you are your own safety net, you can hold all the icky feelings in your body and still be okay.

Can you imagine how different life might be if you were no longer at the mercy of external factors - your own emotions, other people's opinions, world events? Can you taste the sweetness of that level of self-trust? Can you feel the warmth of the deep and true wellbeing that would give you? That's exactly what happens when you regulate your nervous system and deal with the energetics underneath what's going on for you.

It's absolutely blissful. You may have a different word for it, but the feeling is likely to be the same. A calm steadiness in your stomach, a peaceful feeling in your mind. A lot less mental chatter and nasty self-talk, as well as a feeling of being good enough no matter what anyone else thinks, says or does.

That's the point of personal power and, for me, the true meaning of empowerment. The impact of being able to do this for yourself is immeasurable. Had I not chosen to bet on myself and do this work, I would have missed out on the last two years of my life, and that would have been my biggest loss so far.

Neither me nor my dog Boss would have been able to see my parents every day and I wouldn't have been able to be here and give Mr Boss so many beautiful memories with Grandma and Grandad before he passed. I wouldn't have been able to help care for my Dad in the last few months of his life either. As huge as these two losses were, they were also a massive privilege to hold space for and witness. I have so many utterly beautiful memories to take with me throughout my next chapters and there is not one ounce of regret about coming back.

Life for me now is intentionally crafted; it's peaceful AND playful, safe AND spontaneous. The best part by far is that I have the privilege of helping other people achieve their version of bliss. I do this in various ways. I go live on social media every day to show people how to do EFT tapping and give them a sample of my energy and how I do it. This has been the best thing for my business bar none. I fully believe that when you approach business with an open heart and solid non-attachment, magic happens. As a result I have the most beautiful community of souls who I love deeply and who support me unendingly. For those who want to take it further, I have a range of lower cost ways to get my help, like online courses and short group programmes. My all time biggest passion however is teaching Emotional Freedom Technique.

Something happened to me the day I began my practitioner training. My energy responded like an excitable but devoted puppy and I knew that this was what I came here to do. I had always been mediocre at a lot of stuff. Sometimes through a lack of aptitude and other times due to lack of application. EFT was a completely different story. I somehow just knew how to use this to get incredible effects. From day one. It was like my body and energy was remembering something long forgotten.

I qualified as a Master Practitioner in 2015, again in 2016 and as a Trainer in 2017. I began my teaching journey by doing everything the gurus said not to do. I taught online at a time it was not done by many others, because I found connection through the screen just as easy as being in the same room. I began growing my entire business based on group work and memberships. The gurus will tell you to start with 1:1 and then go to groups. I find group sessions to be so very powerful, and I was able to grasp the gossamer thread that linked everybody and follow that to provide relief to everyone's struggles.

As time went on, I met an incredible business coach and certified with her to be a Conscious Business Consultant. Within her certification there was another energy clearing modality called Conscious Energy Clearing. Once again, I felt like I had come home. I loved every bit of it, and the shifts my clients got were nothing short of seismic. I mentioned that I was using the codes with EFT to incredible effect and the next thing I know, she approached me to form a partnership to develop our own modality! Enter Energetic Expansion™.

I have combined EFT and the Conscious Energy Clearing and developed my own end to end process and clearing protocols to leave clients feeling completely safe at the end of a session. When you're not accustomed to energy healing, the code process can feel a little out there. It can bring up things that don't make sense to your conscious mind, in the moment. Energetic Expansion helps prepare your mind, body and energy system to receive the clearing, and brings you out the other side beautifully regulated and calm. None of this would have been possible had I not dealt with the roots of my worthiness issues. I'm grateful for everything that's happened too because, without it, I may still be stuck in the same loop.

Here are 3 principles I live by that you can take with you, if they resonate. They are summed up beautifully in quotes I have gathered over the years.

1. "Until you make the unconscious conscious, it will direct your life and you will call it fate." Carl Jung. In order to make a change in your life, you need to explore the reasons you are doing, or not doing, things. Most of the time, those reasons are unbeknown to us and the best way to get to them is using energy work like EFT and Energetic Expansion. It doesn't dredge up painful emotions and make you relive them, traumatising you all over again. Instead, it works quickly and powerfully to dissolve the connection between the upsetting thoughts you keep thinking and the reaction it creates in the body and mind. So instead of pushing and striving to change a behaviour or pattern, it simply falls away instead. Doesn't that sound amazing?

2. "Without the heart, there can be no understanding between the hand and the mind." Fritz Lang (adapted). This is so key to self trust and empowerment. The heart is a brain in and of itself, and has a signal that is 5000 times stronger than that of the brain. When we come into heart brain coherence, through a focused state of gratitude, love, compassion or empathy, we bestow a multitude of benefits on the body and energy system. Brain waves slow down and you relax more. The nervous system becomes more regulated. Our immune function improves, and much more. Check out HeartMath.com for details on how to do this.

3. "If you want to find the secrets of the universe, think in terms of energy, frequency and vibration." Nikola Tesla. Learn to understand frequency and vibration and the entire universe opens up to you. Learn to master your own and you can co-create anything you desire.

You have everything you need inside of you to shift your reality now, if you want to. Nobody can make that decision for you of course and staying where you are still also a valid decision. Just know that you don't have to spend years in therapy to feel better. You can see, hear, feel, smell, touch, taste, and experience change today. It's all quite literally at your fingertips. Let me show you the way.

ABOUT THE AUTHOR

EMMA STARLING

Emma Starling is a Subconscious Transformation Expert, Business Mentor, Author and Accredited Master Trainer in EFT who works with Joyful Disruptors of the Coaching, Healing and Wellness world. She helps them to dissolve the deepest roots of their self doubt and build unshakeable self-trust, then trains them in a powerful new modality to get the same results for their clients, so they can stand out in their industry as the go-to expert and leave a legacy.

She is an Accredited Master Trainer in Emotional Freedom Technique and Creator of the Energetic Expansion Method and is an author. She lives in North Lincolnshire with her legendary geriatric Rottweiler, Mr Boss where they love exploring the local countryside and enjoying dog friendly venues for afternoon tea. Emma is passionate about spreading the healing ripple and goes live every weekday to teach people how to do basic EFT for free.

Website - www.emmastarling.com
Free Tapping Guide - https://inner-smile.newzenler.com/f/7-steps-to-calm-1

Facebook Business Page - www.facebook.com/innersmilecoach

5

JULIE MAIGRET SHAPIRO

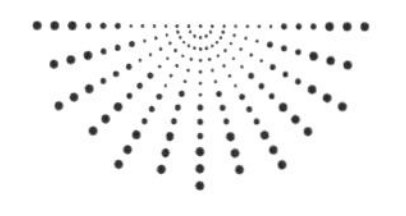

FOLLOWING MY YES

FAMILY MATTERS

I remember the day that everything changed for me.

I am seven years old. When I get home from school, I walk into the kitchen. My mother is standing at the stove preparing dinner. She smiles at me as I perch myself on a built-in counter in the sun. I look out the window and see the majestic view of the San Francisco Bay. Sitting in the window and daydreaming is heaven for me. An only child, I am used to spending a lot of time alone, and my imaginary world is rich. The kitchen is my favorite place to be – especially at this time of day when my mother is making dinner. I lie back and absorb the warmth of the sun. My mother lets me snack on whatever I want – even though my father tells me not to eat between meals. She and I have an understanding.

I love watching my mother in the kitchen. When she's cooking, she comes alive. She throws herself into preparing each dish with such love and determination. I watch her carefully select each ingredient and am delighted when she invites me to sample what she is making. My mother rarely uses recipes. She starts with an idea and then improvises. She moves gracefully from dish to dish in absolute flow. It's like watching a magician concoct a mysterious potion. Her creations always come together beautifully. I am in awe of her skill.

My father is a well-known therapist with a private practice in Berkeley. He works long hours – often seeing 10 to 13 patients per day. Usually, he works until 7:00 pm or later, but today he comes home early. He seems grumpy. My mother and I are experts at assessing his moods. We know when it's best to leave him alone.

He walks into the kitchen and he starts opening the cupboards. My mother and I watch him.

I wonder what he is looking for. After searching through a few shelves, he looks distressed. "Where is my chocolate bar?" he demands, turning towards my mother. My mother shoots me a nervous look.

My mother is heavy. She gained a lot of weight during her pregnancy with me and is about 70 pounds overweight. She is self-conscious of her weight and is always on some diet or another. I hold my breath anticipating the fight between my parents when my mother admits to eating the chocolate bar. My father will be furious with her for breaking her diet and eating his chocolate. My dad has a hot temper! His unpredictable outbursts terrify me. I know to keep my distance when he is angry.

What happens next surprises me. My father starts yelling, "Who ate my chocolate bar?" He turns to my mother. "You ate it, didn't you?"

he shouts. My mother looks flustered. She hesitates, looks down, and then says, "Julie ate it." Stunned, I feel my throat tighten. What just happened? I try to make sense of it. They both look at me, and my father leans in and asks: "Julie, did you eat my chocolate bar?" I know that I didn't eat his candy bar. I can't understand why my mother wants to pin it on me. While I am terrified and confused, I know what to do. I somehow manage to answer in a shaky voice: "Daddy, I ate your chocolate." Then I shrink back, imagining the rage that is coming my way. Instead, my father says nothing. He looks suspiciously at my mother. He starts to say something and then leaves the room in a huff. Still in shock at what happened, I am relieved we made it through that tense moment without him yelling at me.

ROLES REVERSED

After this experience, something changed in our family dynamic. In my mind, the fact that my mother was willing to blame me for something she had done was evidence that she desperately needed my protection. From that moment on, I took on the role of being the family peacekeeper. My job was to keep my parents from fighting with each other. I wanted them to get along and be happy.

Despite my parents' rocky relationship, most of my early childhood memories are positive.

I grew up on a beautiful private road: Maybeck Twin Drive, named after a local and celebrated architect, Bernard Maybeck. Our mid-century modern home was stunning: an architect's dream with dramatic views of the San Francisco Bay. Julian Taylor, an architect, and student of Maybeck, designed it for my newly married parents. It was built of redwood with an indoor-outdoor flow, featuring four decks, French doors, and large windows everywhere. It was the perfect house for entertaining. My parents often threw glamorous parties – in the style of the tv show "Mad Men" with cigarettes, cocktails, and wild dancing...

I was an only child with a lot of energy. A bit of a tomboy, I played in the dirt and ran up and down the hills of our private road all day with the neighborhood kids. I also spent a lot of time reading, making art, and playing with my toys. I had a vivid imagination and my favorite pastime was fantasizing about my make-believe family. I imagined that I was part of a big family with brothers and sisters and parents who were loving, uncomplicated, and got along well.

In reality, my family was small, and my parents were complicated. Both intellectuals in their own right – and each wounded from childhood traumas. In my father's case, he was the youngest son of a family of Jewish immigrants from New York with a mother who didn't respect boundaries. He said he came to California to escape NY baseball mania – but I knew it was to distance himself from his overbearing mother. My mother's abusive French-Canadian father abandoned her and her mother when she was 10. After that, she had to deal with her jealous and inappropriate stepfather. She always felt like an outsider in her family.

Sparks flew when my parents got together at the University of California Berkeley. My mother was an undergraduate, and my father – who was older – was a Ph.D. student. Both were very good-looking, fiery, and sexy. Theirs was an instant connection.

My parents were social, generous, and loved to entertain. They were thrill-seekers who drove convertible sports cars and raced them on the weekends. They entertained frequently – inviting a mix of intellectuals and younger hippie friends to join them – often late into the night. At the time, my parents seemed slightly unconventional and wild. One minute they fought terribly, and the next minute everything was ok. Given their lack of consistency, I learned to be vigilant and read the room.

Within my parents' intense dynamic, there wasn't room for my needs and emotions, so I curbed them instead of expressing them. They both had big personalities and could be overbearing and volatile. With their drama surrounding me, I learned not to take up too much emotional space. Instead, I developed superpowers that worked within their dynamic: I became independent, self-reliant, and emotionally attuned to their moods. I did my best to take on the role of the adult. Someone had to be the steady, responsible one!

My father was bright, handsome, and charming to the world, yet he was often emotionally distant, self-involved, and irritable at home. Deep down, I knew that he loved me. He could be fun and playful when in a good mood. However, those moments seemed few and far between. His compulsive womanizing crushed my mother's confidence and made me feel I had to compete for his love and attention.

His impossibly high standards intimidated me. I never felt I could measure up, yet I still tried to win his approval. My need to strive for perfection was born from this unhealthy dynamic. My father's unpredictable and often explosive anger made me hesitant to approach him. I never knew what would set him off.

My mother was warm, loving, and indulgent towards me. At the same time, she was fragile and needy. She relied on me emotionally since my father wasn't there for her. When my parents' marriage ended, she saw me as her sole source of love and support. She centered her world around me, creating a co-dependent bond.

Honestly, I was ashamed of my family. My parents liked to joke that we were like "The Little Brute Family" (characters from a children's book by Russell Hoban who are ugly, grumpy, mean beast-like animals who eat "sand and gravel porridge" and never say "please" or "thank you.”) I didn't find this funny. It saddened me to think that my family wasn't normal. I believed normal families were kind and got along well all day long. I was determined to fit in and not stand out. My need to belong caused me to diminish any behavior or feelings that didn't conform with my idea of "normal." Keeping up this facade came at a high price. It made it impossible for me to feel at ease.

The coping mechanisms I learned in childhood continued throughout my adult life. I became a master at tending to others' needs before my own. I was good at getting into relationships but found it difficult to set boundaries and speak up for myself. My people-pleasing led to relationships that were unhealthy and unsatisfying. Perfectionism became my go-to strategy to deal with my anxiety about not being good enough or worthy of attention. My work rewarded my self-sacrificing tendencies; however, my perfectionism often made completing simple tasks unnecessarily stressful. Since it was vital for me to be successful at everything I did – I avoided doing anything I might not excel at. My overly cautious behavior limited my options and kept me in my comfort zone.

My mother and I didn't speak about the "chocolate incident" until many years later. I now see how what happened that day profoundly changed my behavior. I could no longer be the child. From that day on, I became my mother's keeper.

After the chocolate bar episode and similar events where my parents overruled my judgment, I had difficulty trusting myself and my decisions.

THE MORE I GIVE, THE LESS I GET

My father died when I was twenty-seven, and losing him made me reflect on my childhood. I started recognizing patterns and beliefs that kept me stuck. As my awareness grew, I began untangling myself from these dysfunctional behaviors that no longer served me. Little by little, things started improving for me. I got a job at a prestigious local university, where I thrived professionally. Things were going my way. I was ambitious and driven to keep moving ahead. I poured all my energy into my work and being a caregiver to my ailing mother. I thought I could do it all on my own. I had no time for myself, but that seemed acceptable to me. Wasn't "busy" the new normal? I just wanted to keep moving forward.

Then in 2016, on a business trip to the Middle East, the cracks started to emerge. It was a successful trip, but the days were long, and the travel schedule was grueling. I was exhausted during the entire trip, yet I kept pushing myself to keep going.

I felt physically, emotionally, and mentally depleted when I returned home. Thoroughly drained, my mood had taken a considerable dip. It felt like a black cloud surrounded me wherever I went. It soon became apparent that I had lost all perspective since everything I experienced was negative. I felt prickly and vulnerable. It felt like an attack if someone said anything slightly critical to me. I couldn't see anything positive in my world. Taking care of my mother felt burdensome and overwhelming. I knew I was in trouble and would sink even deeper into despair if I didn't get support. I decided to ask for help.

After enlisting a team of trusted professionals, I focused on healing my body and mind. I began getting massages and other healing treatments, going to the gym and working out with a trainer, doing yoga, and eating healthfully to regain my energy and vitality. Most importantly, I started making time for myself. It was the first time in a long time that I had prioritized myself. I had gotten so used to neglecting my needs that it was profoundly fulfilling once I began to care for myself. I realized how essential it was to my well-being.

Reviewing my priorities, I realized I needed more time for relaxation. In addition to my rigorous workdays, I was working nights and weekends and had no free time. I started to set boundaries at work. I also realized that I needed support with my caregiving responsibilities. Hiring caregivers for my mother ensured that she got more attention and afforded me more time to relax and recharge. Once I had time for myself, I realized how lonely I was. I had been so busy working and caring for everyone else's needs that I hadn't made time for my social life and having fun. I resolved to change that immediately.

CREATING A NEW NARRATIVE

In 2021, I launched my coaching business: "Women who stay in the game," to help midlife women find their passion and purpose and flourish in their careers. New to marketing and self-promotion, I joined a community of women entrepreneurs and began to learn how to get my message out into the world. I also started writing. I wrote stories in several books. Just by showing up, I found that people responded to my new energy and more authentic persona. For the first time, I received invitations to be on podcasts, give keynote talks, and teach classes. It was thrilling! I had big dreams and thought, "This is my turning point."

Despite my self-awareness and the many positive changes I had made, I noticed that one self-defeating pattern persisted. I was saying "yes" to bold, new experiences; for example, I would say yes to being a guest on a podcast. Nevertheless, I wouldn't take the steps to schedule it and follow through – so it would never happen. I realized that there was a part of me that desperately wanted to grow and uplevel. However, as soon as I imagined a bigger life, "Little Julie" from my childhood would appear with her fears of standing out and would keep me from moving forward. "Little Julie" was sabotaging my growth and big dreams because she felt safer with the status quo. I recognized my imposter syndrome was related to what I had experienced in childhood. Within my family, it didn't feel safe to stand out or trust in myself and my judgment. That part of me still believed that I did not belong in the spotlight. Looking back, I now see that nearly all of my career roles focused on supporting and showcasing other people and their work. It was familiar for me to stay behind the scenes and let others assume the starring roles.

I have healed many of my childhood wounds, including forgiving my parents for putting me in the position of peacemaker and protector. I know they were doing the best they could at the time. Overcoming my childhood patterns and creating a new narrative is an ongoing journey. I feel ready to stop hiding and share my work with the world. It is time for me to be visible and make my mark.

MY YEAR OF YES

Each year I choose a one-word theme for my year. This year I thought long and hard about what word that would be. I named 2023 "My year of yes." I will say “yes” to opportunities that take me where I want to go and “no” to those that don't. I will fully say “yes” with my mind and body. I will not let my fear dominate me or hold me back. This year is about staying open to growth, abundance, possibility and pushing myself outside my comfort zone.

Here's what I have said yes to so far:

- Going back to dating after a long hiatus
- A budding romantic relationship
- Working with more coaching clients
- Letting go of a job where I was playing small and not stretching myself
- Pursuing bigger career opportunities
- Writing this chapter
- Launching a new community for midlife women looking to find soul-purpose work
- Letting go of perfectionism

Saying “yes” to life means staying open to possibilities, taking advantage of opportunities, and displacing my fears with action. I will focus on my strengths and combat my fears to be true to myself, my family, my friends, and my colleagues. I know who I am. I am a capable, strong, intelligent woman. 2023 is my year to take up space, speak my truth and share my gifts with the world. I choose to be the author of my own beautiful life.

YOUR YEAR OF YES

If you are someone with a big vision for your life and need help getting started or staying the course, here is a 3-step process that you can use to dive into your year of yes.

Step 1: Stepping into the mindset of yes

- Get crystal clear on what you want to say "yes" to
- Write out your vision in exquisite detail
- After writing out your vision, put the paper away for a night or two
- Revisit what you have written when you feel ready
- Make sure that everything you wrote truly resonates with you
- Your vision should be what YOU desire - not what others expect from you
- After that, start to visualize your dreams coming true
- Imagine what it would look and feel like to have what you desire
- Who must you be to say "yes" to this life?
- Take a few minutes each morning to visualize your new life

Step 2: Navigate around your fears and objectives

- Write down any fears or objections that surface

- Read over your list of objections and concerns

- Are some of these fears or limiting beliefs? Decide if you are ready to let them go

- If some fears persist, assess whether the fear is a story from your past that is no longer relevant

- Can you acknowledge it and move forward, regardless?

Step 3: Take inspired action

- It's time to take action

- Determine one small step to begin with

- Now, make it even smaller

- Choose something you can do in five minutes or less

- Continue to take small and consistent actions towards your goal to gain momentum

- Do this by connecting with joy and curiosity

- Start experimenting with saying "yes" to small things: a new dish at a restaurant, wearing a unique clothing style, taking a different route to work. Have fun with this!

- Next, it is time to receive

- Stay open to what shows up and celebrate even the smallest wins

- As you welcome small wins – you'll see that bigger wins begin to appear
- Keep saying "yes" and notice what arrives

The one thing that I want you to know is that you are the author of your life story. You get to choose what you want your life to become. I look forward to hearing about all the magic you create by saying “yes” to your desires.

ABOUT THE AUTHOR

JULIE MAIGRET SHAPIRO

Julie founded "Women Who Stay in the Game" to inspire midlife women to find their purpose and share their unique gifts.

Julie works with women who feel called to go after their dreams and make an impact in the world. She helps them rediscover their passion and create more fulfilling careers.

Julie worked as a Learning and Development leader for 15 years. She holds a Bachelor's from UC Berkeley, a Master's from Middlebury College and is a certified executive coach from the Berkeley Executive Coaching Institute. Julie lives in Berkeley, California. She loves to travel and has lived in Italy, France, and Spain and speaks 4 languages.

Julie's social media:
Instagram: https://www.instagram.com/womenwhostayinthegame/
FB: https://www.facebook.com/womenwhostayinthegame
LinkedIn: https://www.linkedin.com/in/juliejmshapiro/
Website: http://WomenWhoStayintheGame.com

6

LAURA KANE

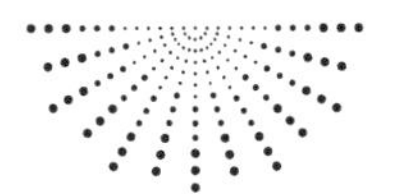

IT'S NOT YOU, IT'S YOUR PROGRAMMING

You may be reading this book looking for answers. Or maybe you're someone who follows me online and you'd like to know the gory details of the wounds from my past I have alluded to. Whatever reason you have for stumbling across these pages,my intention is that you find yourself in them and I hope they bring you strength and inspiration.

How it all started...

My own quest for answers to the question "why am I like this?" is the reason I am sitting here now speaking to you through this book, as someone who today, in her business, finds those answers for others and helps them rapidly heal from the past.

I first want you to know that you are not alone if you have a pattern repeating in your life that is draining you every day, or pops up every time things seem to be going well. Maybe it is anxiety, depression, procrastinating, overthinking or overwhelm. Maybe you feel like an extra in your life and not the main character. You are also not alone if you are currently at rock bottom. I've been there too.

But I want to immediately give you the relief of knowing that patterns can end, quickly. Your rock bottom can be a launch pad for the best that is yet to come.

Let's start with my rock bottom moment, shall we?

In 2019, I had just moved into a stunning, detached, four bedroom home. The sort of home that traditionally, especially where I am from in Northern Ireland, you move into with a family, or at least a partner. I remember my uncle coming to help me with some electrical fittings and saying "you need a family in here".

A few months before this point I had thought that there was at least hope of that happening. I was in a relationship at the time and after a pattern of the same person in a different body entering my life only to painfully leave again, this one was looking good.

I was attending counselling at the time in an effort to heal my internal issues. I knew I had abandonment wounds because this played out in my relationships. In friendships I was never the first to suggest going out in case people said no. In my romantic relationships I seemed to attract people who abandoned me in one way or the other. I also tested partners by pushing them away to see if they would stay or go. At age 32, I was now desperate to ensure this one would work out and I would have the husband and kids I pined for.

I had done "the work" too

You're probably familiar with the narrative that we all have to do "the work" and then we will be healed. We must be healing all the time, it's a constant process, apparently. Well at this point I had done £40,000 worth of that work. Yes, you read that right.

I had done counselling, reiki, life coaching, law of attraction courses, retreats, hypnosis, mindfulness workshops, meditations, you name it, and I had done it. I looked after myself with yoga, pilates and workouts. I ate healthy food as much as possible. I took vitamins and supplements.

But I still had chronic migraine, fatigue, palpitations, mood swings, anxiety, depression, extreme PMS and many tearful conversations with my then partner and frequent arguments with my family.

I was heartbroken moving into this house.

Just a couple of months before, while I was in the middle of selling my old house and buying a new build home (statistically one of the most stressful things humans can do) I was dumped by text. My partner and I had been long distance after he moved away for work. My unhealed inner child took that as him abandoning me. The final straw was a poor connection on a video call, and an argument started from frustration. It was then that I received the text.

"I can't do this anymore".

I went straight into panic mode and of course tried to salvage things. But it didn't work.

I became so depressed in the few months before moving that my friends had to physically help me move. I left things to the last minute because it wasn't how I had planned. I was filled with resistance to move on with my life because the plan was that he would help me and I would have a partner to support me at this stressful time. I didn't like it when things didn't go to plan because it made me feel out of control.

I saw him once before I moved. The only thing he did was take a curtain pole down and leave some cardboard boxes he had sourced on top of my outside bin while I was out. He also told me that I wasn't emotionally stable enough to have my little 10-week-old puppy, Reina, who came into my life on Valentine's Day shortly after the dumping by text. My little godsend who gave me a reason to laugh and cheered me up when I cried.

Moving ended up going well. I had a team of three very friendly movers. They were so nice and so helpful that I felt supported that day at least. My friend Frances was there and she helped mind Reina.

I did it, I pulled through, as I always did.

But the first year in my house felt like I had not really moved in. It was like I was refusing to settle. Refusing to admit that I was there all alone. I even got a job in England briefly and planned to rent it out, until the pandemic hit and I moved back home.

Breakdown, or breakthrough?

Like so many of us, it was in those moments of pure, excruciating isolation in lockdown that I had my breakthrough. Many would call it a breakdown. But I really believe, and I tell my clients this, that these so-called breakdowns are our real selves letting us know they've had enough of the façade. Enough of pretending to be ok. Enough of the job we hate or the relationship we are settling for.

I had been really isolating myself. More than the restrictions forced me to. I didn't so much as speak to another man for a year after I got that text. Dating was out of the question for me. It was almost like, do you know when some food has made you sick, and your body goes off food completely until it has gotten rid of whatever was in your system making you ill?

Well something, somewhere in me was doing that. It was the purge.

Then came the lightbulb moment.

I was standing at the microwave, cooking some sort of meal for one (random I know) and I heard my inner voice speak to me.

Here is what it said:

You're hypnotised by this heartbreak, and you need to be unhypnotised".

It really was a pivotal moment that I remember so clearly because I was at rock bottom. Even though I had a beautiful home, great figure, high paying job in consumer law and regulation, friends, car, holidays, nights out and spa trips and a designer cat and dog to match my décor, I was the most miserable I had ever been.

"Hypnosis you say?" I spoke back to this voice in my mind. "Ok, I'm willing to try anything at this point". So off I went, onto the internet, looking for the cure.

Now if you know me, you know that I don't do anything by halves. I am also effortlessly attracted to the most premium, expensive stuff. I get this trait from my late mother, Eithne, who I lost when I was 28. She had an illness called Huntington's disease, which in the past was known as the Devil's disease, because it is so cruel.

But in my memories of her, I remember her always picking the most expensive dish on the menu when her, Dad and I were out for dinner. Dad found this lovable and funny. "Well what will it be this time, monkfish?" he laughed. Of course, it was. That one was around £18.95 which was a lot of money back then (and even now) for a main course. I mentally marked this as a positive trait. Expensive taste is a trait that has mostly served me well.It was the search for something quality, something high end, that led me to renowned therapist, Marisa Peer, the founder of Rapid Transformational Therapy®. My analytical and critical mind was assessing it all, trying to work out of it was the real deal. Celebrity therapist, check. Wears a Chanel necklace, check. Seems very caring and genuine, check. Marisa felt like the mother figure I never had because the illness had slowly been robbing my mother of her ability to care for me ever since I was born.

I did my research on this therapy. I saw that it wasn't just hypnosis but it used a variety of the best elements from the most up-to-date therapeutic methods while communicating directly with the subconscious mind where all the roots of our issues are stored. Still slightly suspicious, I decided I would go with my gut and have a session.

My life changed in an instant

The message in my mind was one hundred percent correct.

The session I had focused on how I had been subconsciously programmed to not feel enough. This was a new concept to me and I wasn't really sure what it meant. It was explained to me as a universal belief that we all have to some degree which impacts our confidence, self love, relationships and even what we can earn.

I can only describe what happened in that session as therapeutic time travel.

In a matter of moments, boom. I felt a pang of hunger hit my stomach. All I could think of was the Marks and Spencer's food in the fridge. "See, I told you, just like all the other stuff, this isn't working" my critical mind was telling me.

But all of a sudden, an image came into my mind. I knew with absolute certainty that I was aged three. I was sitting in the living room literally starving. I could see my mum pacing backwards and forwards in a vacant manner. These were symptoms of her illness that had not yet been picked up.

No one in my family actually knew, but she was forgetting to feed me.

I recalled not being able to verbalise what I needed, which makes sense because I was three.

Then we left that memory and I was transported, by my own mind, to another.

My brother's death.

I am warning you now that this is even more triggering than the last memory, so you may want to skip a page if you don't want to read this.

I was age 10 and my favourite person on the planet, my eldest brother Austin, had taken his own life.

My dad, a country man who was into hunting, had a rifle. I personally don't agree with hunting, but it was sort of a way of life for the Kane men of that generation coming from a farm.

Austin had taken my dad's rifle and went down to the garden shed and turned that gun on his stomach.

It was me who found him, his head and torso lying flat on the ground at the shed door.

It must have been some divine intervention that I couldn't actually see what the problem was. My first thought was that he had been in the old, dilapidated shed searching for something and fallen and hurt himself.

That day, it was a cold crisp January morning in Belfast. We had two Labradors at the time, they were the ones who woke me by barking at around 10am. I thought this was incredibly alarming as they were working gun dogs, trained not to bark.

The moment I heard them I remember being propelled up from my bed. I had been still asleep in my little box room bedroom which was covered, floor to ceiling with "Forever Friends" teddy bear décor.

It was like I had an electric shock, I sat bolt upright and gasped. Sort of like that moment when you wake from a nightmare, but this nightmare was just beginning.

I ran into the garden past my mother who, shockingly, had not noticed any of this even though she was in the kitchen overlooking the garden. She was just doing that vacant, pacing thing again except this time she was even more gone.

I got to the top of the path leading to the shed and stopped dead when I saw Austin. I was about 5 metres from him. The frenzied way the dogs were trying to get at him through the wire fence of their pen told me something was seriously wrong. "The dogs are worried about him" I thought. I knew from how pale he was that this was an emergency. I noticed that he was just staring into the sky vacantly.

I ran into the house and called 999.

Then I phoned Dad who was working in his newsagents shop in town.

I had the wherewithal to go get our next-door neighbour who was a nurse.

I recall she asked me to get blankets, so I went into the drawers of my room and got two lovely cream wool blankets. The loose knit soft wool ones with the little square holes in them with satin cuffs on each end.

I never saw those blankets again and I never saw my brother again. Except at the wake in his coffin. It was that same week that Mum got diagnosed with Huntington's disease because when she finally realised her son was gone, her symptoms got so bad that Dad took her to hospital. He returned with the news that this was genetic and that I had a 50/50 chance of getting it.

It was on the day I had that session that I realised that none of what had been plaguing me over the years was anything to do with my boyfriends, my job, my friends, my bank account, the economy. None of that.

It started when I was age three and because I wasn't even getting my basic needs met, I had decided that I was not good enough and not lovable. Tiny me had interpreted my mother's vacuous demeanour as rejection.

Then when my best friend and protector Austin left the earth, the one who taught me to cook spaghetti bolognese and told me to wash my hands after petting the dogs before I ate cheese slices out of the fridge. The one who looked after me like a father amidst the chaos. When he left planet earth, I realised that I had interpreted that as him abandoning me. My child mind had thought "but if he really loved me, he would have stayed".

All of that was the root cause of my anxiety, my depression and attracting all of these men that never treated me like I was enough or ended up abandoning me. What astounded me was that in that session, nothing about my ex came up. Or any of the other exes over the years. They were irrelevant.

I realised that the week when Austin died and Mum got her diagnosis was the week my young, overwhelmed mind started to run a worst-case scenario, anxiety-ridden, negative programme. It seemed safer that way. At least if I didn't expect the best for myself, I wouldn't be disappointed. I would later find out after Mum died that I didn't have the Huntington's gene, which was great news, but after getting this letter to say I was in the clear, I was baffled and heartbroken as to why this hadn't fixed all of my issues.

I finally understood the root cause of how I had been feeling, thinking, behaving and what I had been unconsciously creating in my life.

That was the moment that changed my life. Not the £40,000 I had already spent. But that one session of Rapid Transformational Therapy®.

After the session I went straight to the fridge and ate all of the Marks and Spencer's treats.I felt elated and like a massive boulder that had been inside my chest and stomach was gone. I ate so much that day and then I got a stomach upset, which I assumed was all the food.

But what I realised was that yes, I had eaten too much but that was me feeding myself. That was me breaking the cycle of starvation. This was a pattern I realised I had been repeating in my adult life. If a partner fought with me or left me, I literally used to not eat. Then I would binge on junk food. Then I had to do punishing exercise regimes. It was a vicious cycle.

I also realised that my sickness over those two days was my body purging all of the toxins associated with the stress and tension my body had stored for 20 plus years.

I took two days off my corporate job and for the first time I felt no guilt.

Even though my session had nothing to do with smoking, two weeks later I stopped. Just like that. The cigarettes began to repulse me and appear pointless because there was no longer any tight achy feeling in my chest to be relieved.

One by one, toxic and destructive relationships and habits dropped out of my life.

Not long after this I got a promotion to Head of Department at work not because I knew any more information, but because my ability to handle day to day work stress and pressure skyrocketed, and my reaction to stress completely changed too.

The Calling

I had always felt a calling to be some sort of coach or therapist but it was only at this point I felt really ready. I knew that training in the traditional methods of counselling and coaching would not cut it for me. I knew I needed to practice in something that would guarantee a transformation and I knew I first needed to believe that transformation was even possible. After studying Law at university, my first proper job was in Trading Standards, so that consumer protection passion motivated me even further to find a method that would really work and get to the root of people's issues. Having solid evidence that Rapid Transformational Therapy® really did work, having tested it on myself, I decided to train in it.

Today I'm a Holistic Success Coach providing therapy and coaching to ambitious people who are searching for answers as to why unwanted and unhealthy patterns keep popping up for them, holding them back from having the job or business they desire, the relationship they dream of or the healthy body that seems out of reach. It's holistic because these limiting programmes installed in younger life run both in your body and mind. In our healing sessions, together we gently and quickly find and heal the hidden root causes of your symptoms, which allows you to let go of them for good.

I'm so grateful today that I found that method and for the ability it has given me to heal myself and help others heal too. I finally feel like I've transmuted my pain into something positive. It is amazing to me that I am not inherently broken because of all those things that happened in my life. This was something I truly believed from age ten.

So, I guess that is the one thing I want you to know, that you are not broken. But if you feel like you are, it's your programming that is faulty and that can be changed. Heal what switched this programme on in the first place and you'll change your life, no matter how bad it's been so far.

I have even more traumas that I could tell you about, but I am going to stop here because now I want to give you some tips on how you can transform your life too. These are tips I give my clients to help them reprogramme their own minds. Before I get into them, I hope that my story has touched your heart and given you confidence in yourself that you too can transmute your past into something that will empower you every day.

Reprogramme your mind

These are my top five tips to break free of limiting programming and become your real self.

1. Stop being afraid of your emotions

I used to think that if I gave in to the urge to cry that I was weak or headed towards depression again. That's false. Crying releases endorphins and my teacher Marisa Peer told me something quite profound that has stuck with me; "that which can't be expressed in tears will cause other organs to weep". One of the causes of depression and stress is suppressed emotions. So, I really encourage you not to be afraid. Schedule an appointment with yourself for what myself and my Rapid Transformational Therapy® colleagues coined "A mopey day" to really feel your feelings. You can make yourself a little nest on the sofa, stock up on some food and movies and just allow yourself to unapologetically wallow in that emotion. Do whatever you need to do to feel that emotion to completion. You will notice that in a day or two you'll wake up in a different mood, feeling lighter. I believe Beyoncé does something similar by giving herself 24 hours to feel her emotions before moving on like the icon she is. I encourage you to do the same instead of suppressing things.

2. Start and end your day your way

A morning routine is important because of how your subconscious mind works. What many people don't know is that your mind gives you two opportunities daily to reprogramme it. When you wake up and just before you drift into sleep, you are in alpha (hypnosis) brainwaves. This is the same brainwave state I trigger with clients when we are healing the subconscious root cause of their issue. It is a time when your brain is like a sponge, absorbing everything. This is prime programming time! So, if you start or end your day consumed by social media, the news, your boss's emails or some text that has irritated you, then you are programming your mind more negatively. Gratitude and visualising yourself having the life you truly want are great ways to start/end your day. Do this for 30 days and find me online @letgowithlaura, I want to know what happens!

3. Keep your own appointments

You'd be surprised how many busy mums, CEOs and high-level corporate professionals are not making appointments with themselves and not celebrating their wins. To illustrate the impact of this, for just a second I want you to imagine you as a little child. You are trying your best and achieving great things and no one notices.That is how you are treating yourself if you never stop to celebrate how far you've come so far.

If you make appointments with yourself and don't keep them, this is like repeatedly arranging to take eight-year-old you out to the cinema then never showing up. Missing your own appointments whether it is eating healthier food, going for a walk, treating yourself to a nice lunch or coffee or going to that exercise class you said you'd go to is even more damaging to your self-trust. If you want to change your life, you must trust yourself first. You've got to be able to trust that you've got this and you can be comfortable being uncomfortable. So, to start building self-trust today, I encourage you to pick two areas of your life that need your attention and in the next 30 days, make appointments with yourself to improve these areas, and keep them.

4. Your self-talk is public

You'd be surprised at the amount of successful people that have a highly critical and self-destructive inner dialogue.

There are two ways to attain success. By force and by alignment. Many of us use force to berate ourselves if we make a mistake or don't get everything we need to do completed. This is programming received in childhood from caregivers or teachers. But it is important to know that your cells are picking this up, they are responding and vibrating accordingly, so your energetic vibration which is public, is emitting this! I really encourage you to connect with that little inner child version of you and think about how they would like to be spoken to. I'm guessing you are thinking that they want to be given love and encouragement, even if they make a mistake right? Do more of that. This is super important because your thoughts and words are how you programme yourself!

5. Change your inner world and your outer world will match

The number one tip I can give you is that every habit or pattern you have in life, whether good or bad, has a root cause. Psychologically speaking, anxiety, depression, phobias, procrastination, compulsions and addictions are programmes that got installed somewhere along the line as a response to an event or something you learned. They aren't your fault, but they are your responsibility to change. Accessing the real root cause of the things you don't like in your life will set you free the quickest. You don't need to change your world on the outside like moving house or countries, buying the latest trending item or having a nip or tuck.

As long as you're not in an abusive situation, you can stay in the same place, with the same family, and in the same relationship, job and body and feel completely differently about it. In fact, if you're unhappy with your life, before you make a huge change to your physical world, I encourage you to explore your inner world first and let go of what is no longer serving you in there, so that you can start to make your life decisions from a place of alignment rather than from trying to fix your dissatisfaction from the outside in.

To your unlimited success, Laura.

ABOUT THE AUTHOR

LAURA KANE

Laura Kane is a certified Rapid Transformational Therapist®, Hypnotherapist and Success Coach who specialises in helping ambitious people let go of what holds them back and finally enjoy their lives without fear and overthinking. After successfully recovering from anxiety, depression, people pleasing, imposter syndrome and burnout, Laura knew she had to help others gain the same freedom.

Laura has 15 years experience in consumer law and consumer protection and this coupled with a decade of trying various modalities to find the answer to the question "why am I like this", drives Laura to provide people with real life root cause solutions and the answers they too, have been looking for. Laura left a high level corporate position and is now known for her straightforward, empathetic and rapid approach to healing.

Instagram, Facebook and TikTok: @letgowithlaura

Website: www.lauralouisekane.com

7
MARGARET SAP

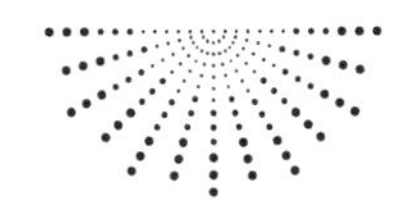

MAKE THE CHOICE - TO USE YOUR VOICE

The impact of contrast

It's a beautiful, soft spring day... I'm sitting on my knees under a blossoming tree. Observing a miracle: a tiny insect.

It moves! It walks. It tries something.

Slowly yet securely.

I don't see what's coming. A shadow suddenly looms over me from behind.

Taking the light out of the sidewalk.

A big shoe.

Splash.

Total shock.

"Kill 'em! They're toxic!" she shouts.

"Horrible creatures! They suck blood out of you."

I look up. Horrified.

At that moment, I sense, without understanding, something crucial:

Truth is debatable.

The shoe is tiny. A size 3 probably.

We're friends, same age, both innocently young.

And our friendship is over.

I instantly lose trust in her.

She does something so rude, so cruel, so sudden.

To a beautiful, now dead, red something on a sidewalk.

She killed a ladybird.

My favorite cute, little garden insect from the picturebooks.

I try to tell her they are harmless.

"That's not true!" she shouts. "Kill 'em all!"

She is convinced she just saved my life as a true heroine.

I have no words to explain my feelings.

I just want to go home.

Understanding

The shock is disrupting.

At this very moment, I become aware of myself as an individual separate from others

It opens my eyes:

Other people see things different than I do.

More incidents follow of course, like in any life.

I learn that people's views and perceptions always differ.

This logical insight leads to

• a free, conscious and worryless way of experiencing relationships with others.

• a well developed human knowledge which becomes invaluable in all areas of my life.

• a pretty non-judgmental way of seeing people. After all, someone does not know what he does not know.

Who am I to judge any of what one might think?

I may have my opinions (ladybirds are cute),

but I can't determine if others have reasons to believe the same thing.

Each human being therefore gets to learn having the humility to understand there's more you don't know than you will ever know and to understand the 'more just righteousness' beyond the civic morality of justice.

The tiny shoe incident is the first moment I remember where sanctity and disaster find each other in a split second, where control and power prevail over my truth and reality.

Contrast

Life is full of contrast over the same thing.

The ladybird example is relative, but concrete proof of it.

Contrast becomes a cherished theme in my life.

I learn to embrace it rather than oppose it and I flow in between both sides with ease:

It's an enriching approach to living as it allows me to guard my heart and deal with something according to the situation, person or purpose, rather than by predestined convictions alone.

If someone thinks differently than me, I'm open to understand their point of view. I like to collect lots of ideas and original ways of thinking to see things in a new light, or validate my own. Thinking about something in a refreshing way, changes my understanding and experience of it too.

But, back to the collective.

If everybody has a different view on reality, then:

What is true, who speaks the truth and if we can't see it, can we find it together?

This is the eternal search for the holy grail.

Throughout history, people fight over competing beliefs and ideologies, often enduring great trials of virtue and faith in order to defend what they hold to be true.

Truth.

Truth is the concept people confuse with what is right or wrong, good or bad, traditional or progressive.

This approach to truth proves to make life unnecessarily hard.

And harsh. For each other.

In situations where truth is not clear-cut and people and cultures have varying ideas about what is true and right, it is challenging to navigate ethical dilemmas. It's then important to consider not just one's own values and *wants*, but also the values and *needs* of others in order to make informed and meaningful choices.

Daily bread

As a child, I'm fed with potatoes, respect and dinner table conversations - witty jokes, bedtime stories and songs. There's not much money, but language is treated like wealth.

This unconscious creative living makes me resilient as it feeds my soul with beauty without me realizing its importance. The qualities of image, music and story function as a trampoline to jump off into the world energetically and with enthusiasm.

Life is good. I live by values that are clear and easy to understand. It's just as it is. In looks, in touch, in time taken to listen and to be listened to.

Choices are made from love and for love, so I grow up in appreciation.

As stewards of an abundant planet we get to take care of each other and the earth, by working towards it, enjoying it and celebrating with gratitude.

As humans, we are creative beings by nature, so we are capable of being lusciously abundant too. To illustrate that, my parents sometimes put an empty chair at the dinner table. Visibly making space for the invisible: unexpected visitors are welcome to have dinner with us.

The value toolkit

Little by little my life's toolkit fills with instruments for heartfelt living: spirituality, honesty, fierceness, creativity, freedom, empathy, modesty, security, team spirit, self expression, trust and last but not least humor!

These immaterial assets require maintenance as regular tools do, to keep them reliable so that you don't sweat the small stuff and support the clutter of pain.

I learn that love is great, yet that respect comes first. In every interaction, it's important to gauge whether mutual respect is present. By doing so, you can ensure that you aren't harmed or taken advantage of under the guise of love.

Weave respect as a red thread through everything you do, as something precious to give and to receive.

In times where choice rights are taken away in postmodern societies and people contend over power and control, it's crucial to read the signs of time. Absence of mutual respect is a red flag: it's crucial to stay vigilant.

Be resilient enough to speak up.

When you are disrespected or humiliation takes place in your presence, ask for clarification. Your health is at stake if you allow disrespectful behavior to creep under your skin, because silence can be a slippery slope towards victimhood.

Voice

Erosion of self-respect pollutes your springs of life. So you have to react to protect your self-love.

Here's where you activate your voice.

Whether softly inside of you, or out loud: You Get To Speak.

You sharpen your self-respect by asking a proper question.

Instead of an emotional why-question, ask:

"What is the purpose of you (__________) me like this?"

Or at least, make an internal whisper.

I had no words to say to the ladybird nor to my friend.

I just valued the insect differently than my friend did.

All I uttered to myself was: I want to go home.

My friend was raised in a different value system.

If everybody lives in their own movie, how can we operate as communities?

Values steer your view on life and in relationship with others require an activated voice to avoid misunderstanding and assumptions.

You get to speak, to express what's most important to you, for the sake of any relationship.

To practice, start with the relationship between you and yourself.

What do you tolerate? What do you hold yourself accountable for?

You choose.

Either you move your life forward by your values.

Or someone else will move your life with theirs.

Still waters

Growing up with heart-led wonder, instilled values guide my choices.

Yet life's not always happy bees buzzing...

Slowly situations become more difficult and tempting.

As a teenager, I get to actively use my moral compass.

I am testing life and how it feels.

Let me tell you, lying feels off.

It takes away my joy.

It's like bird poop on the window through which I look at the world.

My childhood values become important enough to cherish them.

As with character traits, values are not immutable and can always improve.

Like the real tool, your moral needle has to point north

yet needs to stay flexible to be trustworthy.

Movement is key

The rigidity and hypocrisy of immovable civic morality come to mind. I have developed a nose for its inheritance, called pretense.

Like out in the fields, still waters become moisty. It stinks.

That's why a good tempest is so appreciated. It cleanses and stirs life up, mostly for the better.

Life's storms continually test your compass.

Are you doing what is right or, when the going gets tough, what you're told is right?

How do you treat weaker ones when nobody sees you?

To avoid arrogance and resentment, you, your traits and moral convictions require finetuning, because change is natural.

Keep moving. It brings along inspiration and... vitality.

Deeper waters

Once you have your values as tools and anchors on board,

you can move yourself out of shallow water into deeper ones.

There's no time being emotional about growing and moving on.

Emotions are best off when dealt with shortly (note that I don't say hastily), as long as it's with genuine empathy.

Like when I am 12 years old, we're swaying across the country from a wealthy, densely populated area to a financially poor, rural area. No time to cry about it. No chance to imagine what our new house or friends will look like. And that's okay.

Imagination after all - to paraphrase Charles Faulkner - is not about what you think specifically.

More important is *how* you think and I anticipate every move as a new adventure.

A different community has other rules and assumptions and in this case even a different language. It's a big change.

Despite a culture shock, I enjoy the salty air, the smell of grass, the endless view and marvelous sunsets. Growing into adulthood living close to nature, I witness, endure and get shaped along with the weather cycles - as a mystical child with a free spirit.

A playful mind

Yet I carry a treasure, deep within me:

The privilege of knowing that where I am today, here at this place, is only temporary. It makes it special.

Better enjoy what I have now that I'm here. Why bother complaining, if it only makes the road harder? After all, it's not forever.

This flat landscape with a handful of mounds and churches, invites me like a blank canvas to use my imagination. What if I pretend to be a tourist in this region? How will I then value what I see today? I will surely appreciate these cute little farms, the fresh puffy pink clouds, the vastness...

It's this self-invented insight that enhances my life: I discover the power of my mind during the weekly powerful storms that reign these empty spaces.

The gift of vision of another world beyond where I am now turns my current situation into a playing field of possibilities. It makes my days truly more enjoyable.

I experience that it's not the circumstances that define my happiness.

It really is up to me.

Resistance

But also.

I see peers. Resisting to learn, to grow, to change.

Ladybird level shockingly sad.

They don't fly. They don't even try.

Smashed, cracked, depleted before the age of 18.

And so it happens.

My innocent view on life gets infiltrated with the shadow sides of it as well.

Real life stories.

The time for illustration books is seriously over.

I see victimhood playing up in both oppressor as well as in victim.

People, like boats, are drifting and anchors can't be found!

I feel like a bumblebee in the midst of it all.

Shall I engage or shall I ignore it?

Can I change this? Can I add value - or values - here?

Boys dreaming of traveling - but not encouraged to look beyond the horizon.

Girls with potential to learn - yet not invited to think critically.

Girls saying things that make sense - yet only condemned to be pretty.

Boys having big emotions - yet not taught how to express themselves,

... so many drink themselves to splutter.

And I talk and listen to peers and say: You are free!

There's a world beyond your situation. You can't see it, but it's there.

If you don't know it, imagine it!

If you don't choose change now, you are your own biggest oppressor.

It is disheartening:

Even here, where the earth literally lies at the feet of endless skies as one big invitation to come alive, one still can become a slave to circumstances, in contrast: either victimhood or comfort zone.

Life's not a joke

And I think to myself: No way I will spend my one and only life standing still.

As a bike rider, I know: If you stand still, you fall. So mentally I move on and anchor my vision into an unknown future.

Sixteen I am, when I start studying the mind by choosing martial arts as my high school thesis. Powerful minds in trained bodies, arts neatly developed by monks observing insects.

Fighting means being prepared to kill or be killed.

You lose either way.

Therefore, the best fighter will make the wisest choice: to avoid the battle.

Raised in Western spirituality and philosophies, the Eastern versions are as fascinating to me. I absorb the learnings and find many overlaps, which strengthens my belief in universal values over cultural ones.

I learn that taekwondo, kung fu, karate, aikido, etc. all lead to one insight:

Our biggest enemy is not our opponent. It's us, ourselves, due to lack of self control.

I'm still young, when I gasp the notion that life is a continuous evolution into mastering oneself. I come to the conclusion that self-awareness and self-regulation are the only reasonable pure forms of truth we can ever find.

Activation

So the question is: who do you want to be with your values and choice options?

Change happens by making a choice. The choice gets activated when you use your voice.

In martial arts it's the loud "kihap" shout that brings in oxygen.

In spirituality, it's the power of prayer.

In daily life, your soft whisper is the beginning of building strength: I am free.

To be free, you get to choose WANTING to be free.

With that comes the responsibility, so many shy away from.

It's the hidden contrast within the great wor(l)d of freedom.

Freedom is a 'verb'. It requires you to act. To respond.

It invites you to think. It encompasses the right to doubt.

You have the right to choose.

Freedom obviously is not a given, now that even pro-choice ethics require protection - again. It's important to take responsibility and stop taking freedom for granted.

It requires pro-active and engaged protection on various levels and it starts with you.

Tomorrow all may be different.

To free yourself from your circumstances and to advance by choosing change, be guided by Romans 12:2 “Do not conform to the pattern of this world, but be transformed by the renewing of your mind.”

♪♪Imagine all the people living life in peace ♫

Stand up, walk your talk, so that choice starts to work within you.

Be vigilant, to avoid the size 3 shoe, and always be ready to move on.

Choices

The spring of my 18th birthday, I sit on the dyke regularly. Watching.

Shimmering lights over this Unesco World Heritage site called Wadden Sea, Europe’s most precious birthing place of birds and fish.

I see young men, floating on boats in the sun, peacefully. Friends tell me these guys earn a lot of money. It seems like an ideal job, now that high school runs to an end.

After my failed attempt to become a sea dredger, I come up with the idea to swap my bike for riding in style: motorcycle and horse.

So I sign up for the Royal Marechaussee, the military police force of the Kingdom of the Netherlands, while my parents seemingly keep their calm.

The fascinating contrast of revolution (heart) and authority (mind) is appealing to me, as I respect and understand both sides of the medal.

As a highly educated candidate, I'm suddenly invited to join the Royal Military Academy and soon I'm practicing assault courses on an Open Day.

This is where my father steps in. Wisely.

When I come home from school one day, he calls me up in his study room:

"I called an old friend of mine... I asked what experience he thought you'd get as the intelligent girl you are. He thinks you might have a hard time."

The power of positioning at work.

"Either you step into the military as one of few girls among many boys or you go to Amsterdam, where you make friends for life and obtain a university degree."

I can not choose.

"I love the idea of serving the country. You surely understand."

"The most important thing to learn in life is how to make choices well" he reacts.

That remark really pisses me off, because it does not help me. At all.

I want the decision to be easy. This impossible feeling needs to dissipate quickly. Can't he make the choice for me?

More than I do, he knows that I'd probably rally against that either way.

Ruminating at night, victimizing myself in this privileged situation of getting to make a choice for a forward change, I discover that overthinking sucks.

Decisions, emotions, relationships and ideas become tough once you start to overanalyze. What a terrible place to be in. Choosing only becomes more complicated, almost impossible.

And then, thank God, the light bulb goes on:

I am given the gift of trust!

My father has given true support after all!

The best support actually!

Trust.

Any form of judgment or advice would have taken my power away. It would have set me up against him. It would have deflected what this choice was about: My Precious Life.

“You get to choose” indirectly meant that whatever choice forward I would make, it would be okay.

The choice is my response-ability to this gift.

I simply need to become clearer about my vision. And so I did.

Big City Life

A few months later, I arrive in Amsterdam with my delicately painted, old bike.

Curious for change, ready to embrace this metropolis, shy, and just as I am: open.

The bike gets stolen in the first week.

The money I worked for all summer, is gone within two.

In week three, I enter a new world of severe hazing among the rich and wealthy within the most traditional student fraternity.

The contrast with previous years is huge.

The humor, mores and theatrical aspect of every situation I end up in... I find it all hilarious. Challenging tasks are eye opening, missions seemingly impossible are achieved and character strengths are tested for sure. You make friends for life in this pressure cooker.

The second priority, after having fun meeting new friends, is: work.

Work is an absolute privilege when you're in need of money.

I work day and night to fund my education, books, rent, bread, beers and cigarettes and oh yes, sports membership. I work way more hours for a salary than ever sitting at the uni benches, libraries or any other educational institute.

And I trust that one day, I will graduate.

Becoming wiser

Thanks to working in various communities I simultaneously actively engage in, I rapidly discover they all have their own cognitive biases, myself included, and how these influence decision making.

People hear and listen to what they already know and comfortably seek confirmation or validation of what they think over and over again.

In every group, there are people who are bold and not polite, but they use their voice to get what they want. They usually win by using catchy phrases that people can easily understand, even if what they're saying isn't true. This means people don't need to think too hard about what they're hearing. Just hearing it can make them feel emotional and believe it's true. Following secured.

If ever the convincing does not work, the trick card of confusion is played.

I begin to understand how oppressive systems and false hierarchies are changing gradually. It's fascinating and it's what I'm passionate about studying.

Expertise

These hidden societal currents become my focus academically and later on I also apply this knowledge as trend marketeer: Linguistics, cultural science, communication, sociology, philosophy and cultural mentality history.

Not the learn-by-heart date of The French Revolution, but what has been leading up to it. What are the invisible, underground movements that are so defining?

People don't like change and often resist it. Those in power are less likely to want change, while those without power lack the energy and opportunities to pursue change.

Change requires disruption. It starts with people who dare to express their desire for change. With a song, a dress, a video, a tag, a mural, a whisper...

Creativity and its problem solving benefits can disrupt the status quo within movements, institutes and thinking patterns. Is it the reason why art education is not a priority in schools?

I learn how moral beliefs and non-conforming behavior are choices too.

I see people wavering. Comparing. People-pleasing. Faking. Afraid to express themselves, fearing social rejection. People enjoying their achievements, but not having joy in themselves.

Behind the pretense hide so many beautiful true personas.

The sweetest of sweet people end their lives.

And it truly saddens me.

More seeds are planted that lead me to do the work I do today.

Luckily, joy and love reign those years of my life, thanks to a good family bond and really great friends that are in my heart forever.

Work hard, play hard

As a Master of Arts graduate, I start my career in the thriving music industry.

I roll out of my roaring twenties being one of the top 50 senior managers, strategically leading PR teams in over 20 countries, of one of the most renowned sports brands in the world.

Traveling around the globe, I meet high performance athletes, organize fashion shows and events in hot spot cities and work with a large variety of journalists from all sorts of media, fashion stylists, talented street artists and first class music performers.

Yes, I pinch myself regularly.

Above all, I meet wonderful colleagues from all walks of life, blending my love for people and special interest in universal values and intercultural relations (the theme of my MA thesis) with real life experiences.

Trust

My whole career is purely driven by one alternative choice, followed by bliss, enthusiasm and dedication and loving what I do.

Trust is given to me in all positions, which fires up my responsibility. I dare to lead with respect and clear ethics, by bringing happiness, knowledge and opportunities to my teams and network, always by working towards a beautiful vision together.

This approach to harmony makes me flourish:

I love the work I do, hard nuts included, back then and still today.

Self Agency

In 2010, YC More was founded. Why See More.

'Cause there's so much more to life than what your eyes see.

I combine my love for the arts, people and children of the future with my interest in the invisible trends that make individuals and societies grow.

My broad life experience, expertise and various qualifications turn me into a thriving personal leadership and lifestyle coach. It's wonderful to work with people and teams that are eager to discover the multiple benefits of knowing themselves better.

It's a privilege to guide you on the shortest, but most important journey:

The one from your head to your heart, where you find a long forgotten cheerfulness, fueled by your gifts and talents.

Urgency

Co-occurring crises trigger confusion and lead you to places of fear and judgment that simply do not do justice to the beauty of life. It smudges your view.

In a world often misled by distrust and confusion, the one lesson I want you to know is that your best bet is funding trust in who you are becoming by cultivating more awareness, resilience and empathy.

I stand for a planet that is a beautiful place, one that is created and cultivated with love and needs to be nurtured and protected with seeds and deeds of care, joy and possibility. By people just like you.

This is what I wish for you today and for the children of tomorrow:

Green, colorful fields of wildflowers. Abundantly smiling in the wind.

It starts with you whispering: I am purpose. I am free.

You are purposeful with your power of choice to change.

Stop living in fear of the shoe.

Yes, you are vulnerable as a tiny insect.

But resilient as a wildflower. And powerful as a storm

It's no reason to turn against yourself nor another human.

Ever seen ladybirds fighting each other?

Hear the calling to create good, beauty and truth. Three key values that are subjective and in their purity can only be found in your own heart.

Lead from that place of love, listening to the voice that says

"There is no reason to fear; You are not alone."

Be true to yourself. Choose, Change, Trust.

Cheerful Enlightenment will be your reward.

"The real voyage of discovery consists

not in seeking new landscapes, but in having new eyes." -Marcel Proust

---

ABOUT THE AUTHOR

MARGARET SAP

Margaret Sap is a life artist, mentor and author.

Founder of YC More, Margaret coaches high-achieving senior managers who want to upgrade their personal leadership, lifestyle choices and core values, so that they will rejoice at their life. With an MA in linguistics, communication and socio-cultural trends and her 15+ years of experience as Global Brand Strategist and Trend Marketeer for well renowned brands and celebrities, she knows how much the power of words and impact of images affect mentalities and societal norms.

Her courses, coaching and projects are designed to unwind these conventions and support you on the joyful and meaningful journey of self-(re)discovery and self-expression.

Margaret invests in Joy Filled Persons (JFPs) for a living. If you long to live a congruent life as the person you truly want to be(come), she guides you - through your power of choice - to become the inspiring and resilient change agent the future needs - today.

Website: www.ycmore.com
Linktree: https://campsite.bio/margaretsap
Subscribe to Sparks of Joy: https://ycmore.com/sparksofjoy/

8
MARY GOODEN

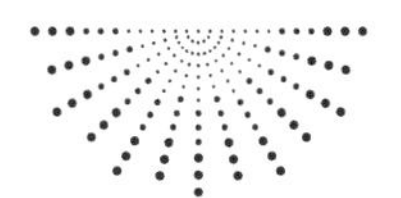

" I AM OPEN TO RECEIVE ALL THAT THE UNIVERSE HAS FOR ME "

I must have recited this mantra over one-hundred times before I fully recognized its power.

I had been playing small. I was shining in my authenticity, delivering my message and walking my talk on a really small platform. A platform that I created. I danced around the vibration of expansion in fear. Fear that I would lose, that I wasn't enough and that my message didn't carry the power of lasting change.

Sound familiar?

The universe is waiting for you!

Not the idea of you, or the you that you were taught to be.

Not the complicated version that makes everyone except for you happy.

Not the pre-programmed version that stops you from saying yes to fun, play and uncertainty.

The you that can only be discovered by honoring, accepting, embracing and loving the wholehearted being that you are.

It is a wild ride.

I dare you to do it!

I dare you to recite the mantra with intention.

Knowing that every desire you have ever had will be delivered to you.

Now, all I desire to do, is to share this amazing gift with you!

I have spent the last 20 years learning, practicing, researching, and mastering the art of living wholeheartedly on purpose.

What does it mean to live wholeheartedly?

Living from a place of inner balance and harmony – an alignment of what you think, feel, say and do. Through my committed effort along with the practice of yoga, meditation and reiki energy harmonizing, I have fully embraced wholehearted living and discovered my soul's mission and purpose. I am willing to share my experience, guidance and love to support and serve you in the most sufficient and fulfilling way, so that you too can live wholeheartedly on purpose.

It all starts with a great mantra, a short statement that echoes in your mind, especially when you start to feel a decline in your energy or vibration. The mantra that I hold close to my heart is, "I am open to receive all that the universe has for me." With faith, hope, and love as my superpowers, my journey has encompassed first-hand experience and research on the benefits of yoga, meditation, and reiki energy harmonizing. These modalities have led me to self-trust, authenticity, enlightenment and purpose. I have been guided to share my experience and support you in discovering, living and sharing yours.

Let's take a deeper look at these modalities and how they are used to reshape your inner world, as well as some of my experiences and enlightening moments.

It all started with a yearning for something different. I loved a tough physical work-out, I was a runner, weightlifter, a real cardio junkie. As I write this now it was more than likely the insatiable need to be enough, high-anxiety and coffee that provided me with an endless amount of energy. I was a mother, workaholic and a work-out addict. I managed a fast-paced, highly profitable business and taught several fitness classes a week. I was delighted to share my knowledge, expertise and energy with anyone who was willing to listen and try new things. My friend Stacey came in to work one day super excited to share her discovery of a new yoga studio and I was all ears! I was always eager to try new experiences and was somewhat familiar with the movement of yoga, so I decided to give it a try. It was truly love at first feel, the energy that filled the space was calm, peaceful and compassionate. Almost immediately this space became the most desirable part of my week. On Sunday night I would take the "Sacred Music" class, it was a 90-minute candlelight flow, the perfect way to prepare for the week ahead and the instructor Kasia was a treasure that will live in my heart forever. I mention this class specifically because this is where I first received the calling to become a yoga instructor. I remember it like it was yesterday, as I begin to awaken from savasana, coming back to consciousness. I knew at that moment that I absolutely wanted to make others feel exactly as I felt, pure, content and at peace with all things. The very next day I sought out a yoga teacher training program that felt right and my journey of self-study was about to blossom.

It is true what you have heard, life is a journey not a destination. In fact, the darkest moments and experiences in our life bring us the most profound growth. I am certainly not suggesting that you seek the dark moments, nor I am saying that if you haven't experienced the darkness that you are not growing. Honestly, I wasn't exposed to what felt like my darkest moment until 2014, however looking back now it was the brightest experience on my path.

Awakening feels awkward most of the time, an instant where the light breaks through the darkness. It is about getting out of your comfort zone and inviting a positive change in the way you perceive your experiences. What I hope to share with you in the practice of yoga, meditation, and reiki energy harmonizing is that you are the creator of your perception, your experiences and your life regardless of external circumstance and limiting beliefs. We are all here to discover and serve a purpose, a personal mission to expose the light not only within ourselves, but in those around us.

Yoga, Meditation and Self-Realization

The practice of yoga is certainly not a new tradition. Hatha yoga has been shown in ancient text to date as far back as 800 years. In what we call the Western world, the first school of Hatha was established in 1918. Yoga is defined as the uniting of the mind, body and spirit, to your higher consciousness, God, Divine, or Source. It has been noted as a healing science, as regular practice will increase awareness and decrease disease. Yoga is a practice of self-study or self-realization. I like to think of it as coming home to yourself. Some of the health benefits of practicing yoga and meditation regularly are:

- Decreases anxiety and helps you release from "fight or flight" mode, creating more time spent in a calm state of peace.
- Encourages a cultivation of non-judgement, self-trust, balanced ego, and genuine kindness.
- Increases flexibility, muscle strength, respiration, circulatory health, along with energy and vitality.

Yoga offers eight limbs or basic guidelines on how to live a meaningful or soulful life. The first four aspects lean in a more practical direction and are designed to prepare you for the second half of the journey, the pathway to Samadhi, described as a pure state of ecstasy. The last four aspects relate to meditation and creating a space for you to hear the whispers of your soul. This part of the journey requires that you fully embody your authenticity.

1. **Yamas** - which follow the golden rule of "treat others as you wish to be treated," drawing focus on your own behavior, nonviolence, truthfulness, non-stealing and non-possessiveness, refining your personality.

2. **Niyamas** - which deal with self-discipline and spiritual practices, purity, contentment, self-study and surrender to your God, Divine or Source.

3. Asana - which relates to the physical practice of postures, developing a relationship with your body and energetic awareness of yourself. The practice of moving the body seamlessly with the breath, learning self-discipline, compassion and acceptance as you meet the body where it is, concentration, and being present which will be useful in meditation.

4. Pranayama - gaining mastery and full awareness of your breath, this is the life force within. The breath is the largest healing system in the body and possibly the one that we take for granted the most. In my experience it isn't unlikely for a doctor, psychologist, or psychiatrist to suggest that you take deep breaths to calm yourself down. I give yoga a standing ovation for teaching me how to breathe! Breath-work can be practiced as an isolated technique; however, it is integral to the physical practice of yoga posture.

5. Pratyahara - meaning detachment from external distraction or sensory transcendence.

6. Dharana - concentration and focus on stilling the internal distractions of the mind.

7. Dhyana - meditation or contemplation, becoming fully aware without any focus.

8. Samadhi - union of self and connection to higher consciousness, to God, Divine, or your Source.
In my opinion, Samadhi is achieved through living authentically and in alignment with your soul's purpose. A blissful experience of

being one with the Universe and fully aware of all the abundance that surrounds you. Through consistent, daily practice, self-acceptance, self-love and self-trust anyone is capable of this experience or enlightenment.

I support my clients fully on this journey to align with their life and business through Anchor Your Light Academy. I work with clients both virtually and in person.

My Anchor Your Light Immersion sets a stage to welcome yourself home. I help you discover your innate ability to create harmony in all areas of your life. I teach the benefits of breath, mantra and meditation as you embark upon your journey toward mindfulness. These offerings are reiki inspired and include connecting to higher self, breath-work, chanting, mantra, emotional freedom tapping, meditation and yoga nidra practices.

My refreshing retreat in Sedona, Arizona is a mindful journey of the heart! A time for reflection, relaxation and rejuvenation for your body, mind and spirit. This all-inclusive retreat will invite you to find clarity, purpose, and freedom. A space to fully immerse in your heart's desire. It includes yoga and meditation, reflection and release activities. Including world-class hikes, vortex visits, outdoor adventures and personal loving support.

Reiki and Chakra Energy Systems

Reiki energy harmonizing/healing is an amazing gift that was shared with me during an interesting time in my journey. I had just made the decision to resign from my position in the corporate carnival and was in need of an energetic reset. My energy body had become aligned with high pressure work ethics and stress inducing strategies. I now hold a master level in this modality, which has been a vital skill that serves to guide and support clients in discovering their inner light and purpose successfully. I offer in-person and virtual seminars, workshops, harmonizing sessions and energy attunement sessions that are loaded with information concerning the energy body for individuals and groups.

Reiki Attunement is the process of transferring the power of universal life force energy to the student by a reiki master. Clients are provided a complete guide on the energy body/chakra system and an open discussion about how chakras impact your life, as well as how to create inner balance and harmony.

Reiki is a "spiritually guided life force energy." This modality takes a holistic approach to harmonizing/healing the body. The technique aids in the reduction of stress and promotes relaxation and healing. It is administered by "laying on hands" and is based on the idea that an unseen "life force energy" flows through us and is what causes us to be alive. If one's "life force energy" is low, then we are more likely to get sick or feel stress, and if it is high, we are more capable of being joyful and healthy. I have thoroughly studied reiki energy along with the chakra energy system for the last decade. A chakra is literally a vortex of energy, connecting our physical existence to higher and deeper non-physical realms. These seven energetic set points in the body act as filters for the experiences that we encounter from past lives all the way to the present moment. What we generate determines much of what we receive, hence the idea of karma. A blockage or imbalance in one or several of the chakras can initiate mental, emotional, physical and spiritual ailments. When properly balanced the seven chakras work together to create the optimal life. I personally use reiki, yoga, crystals, sound healing vibration, and mantra meditation to heal and restore chakra balance. I have a daily practice of praying, visualizing, and aligning my mind, body and spirit so that I may present as the very best version of myself. Each one of the seven chakras are responsible for the emotional and physical energy within a certain point of your body. The following is a map of the chakra location and purpose:

1. The root chakra "Muladhara" is located at the base of the spine and manages your security, stability and assurance.

2. The sacral chakra 'Svadhishthana" located above the root, below the belly button manages your emotional resilience, including guilt, shame, and codependency, along with being a center for creativity and sexuality.

3. The solar plexus chakra "Manipura" is known as the "fire of desire" just above the belly button. This super powered chakra manages self/ego, confidence, acceptance, and self-belief.

4. The heart chakra "Anahata" is located above the solar plexus in the center of the chest. This amazing space of energy, light, and soul expression manages love, compassion, forgiveness, and gratitude. I believe the space of the heart chakra is where your voice of purpose lives. Every morning before I get out of bed, I pause in stillness with both palms on my heart space and listen for the whisper of my soul.

5. The throat chakra "Vishudda" is located in the center of the throat

space. This is where we enliven self-expression, courage and authenticity.

6. The third-eye "Ajna" is our connection to clear thinking, imagination, self-reflection, and intuition. It is nestled in the center of the brain near the pineal gland.

7. The crown chakra "Sahasrara" is your spiritual connection to higher consciousness, God, Divine, or Source. A balanced crown chakra allows you to feel freedom, unity, and complete harmony!

Combining the knowledge and practices of yoga, meditation, reiki, and chakra energy allowed me to truly know myself and in this knowing self-love, self-trust, and self- acceptance anchored and expanded the light of my soul.

Beginning the Journey

Treat this journey the same as you would a new friendship, get excited about it, prepare for new adventures, surrender to the unknown and have fun! When I was running one morning, I was thinking of ways I could encourage clients to embrace this way of life, and this is what I heard:

S.I.M.P.L.E. – Seriously Imagine More Positive Life Experiences!

What is pulling on your heartstrings right now? What in your life is screaming for your attention and transformation? Honor everything that you hear and write it down. On the same piece of paper write down your dreams, your wishes and your desired outcome.

Now, let's pick a mantra to help you eliminate distraction. A mantra encourages you to practice activation of free will, no longer ruled by the seeds of your mind. Practicing a mantra will reduce the mental fluctuations of your mind quickly. If the mind is steady your body will follow. Allow me to share a few that I have used to embody soulful living:

- "Everything I need is already within me"
- "Life is always happening for me"
- "I can achieve anything I desire"
- "I am present in this moment accepting who I am where I am"
- "I love myself, I trust myself, I am enough"
- "Abundance flows to me with ease and grace"

Is there a mantra that resonates with you here? Maybe something is already entertaining your mind that is perfect for you in this moment. Use your mantra as often as possible to bring yourself back to present moment awareness.

Meditate with your mantra. Meditation is not a practice of sitting in a dark room as still as possible, I tried that for a minute and all I could feel was chest pain. Look for guided meditation, offerings that take you on a journey. I have developed specific meditations for my clients based on their individual needs, I would be honored to do this for you too. You can also find some great offerings on YouTube. Yoga nidra specifically works with mantra meditation. This practice is referred to as "yogic sleep," how can you go wrong with that?

Make yourself a yoga date and take your mantra with you! Research some local yoga studios or try a few online if that feels better. If you're a beginner, find a basic class and remember the guidelines of yoga, this practice is a judgment free zone. In my yoga classes I constantly remind my clients that the mind tells the body, and the body responds. I remember my early days on the yoga mat. I used the energy of force to get my body to look a certain way, it was my ego's need to look like my mat neighbor who had been practicing yoga forever.

What I have learned is that force is not necessary, everybody is designed differently, everybody will look different and feel different, so I started embracing my differences. My yoga still teaches me self-love, compassion and trust. What I learn on my mat I live off my mat. If you start to feel distracted or frustrated inwardly repeat your mantra. I make it a point to try everything twice, just in case I missed something the first time. Success lies in your ability to love and accept yourself exactly where you are!

Finally, schedule yourself a reiki or energy harmonizing session. This is a holistic modality that is purely designed to create inner harmony. I understand the dis-ease that is created by unfortunate life circumstances, anxiety infused lifestyles, hopelessness and the need to be free from limiting beliefs. Allow yourself to experience this amazing energetic tune-up.

Some of us have spent our lifetime living in a state of dis-ease. Open your heart, your mind and your soul to receive the gift of this life. Allow yourself to transform, to release from cultural conditioning and live authentically now!

Create a daily practice of making the choice to live in your truth, your love and your purpose. The universe is here to guide you, love you and support your destiny toward wholehearted living.

My mission is to support awakening souls in defining and aligning with their ever-evolving mission and purpose. This human experience is an invitation from the Universe, Mother Earth, the Creator to awaken, the stage has been set, the body, mind and spirit are designed to unite and open the door of your deepest desire, your soul's purpose.

Be brave and move wholeheartedly into what lights you up.

ABOUT THE AUTHOR

MARY GOODEN

Mary Gooden is CEO and founder of Divine Destiny Mentoring & Publishing, the host of Shine Your Soul Light Podcast and a Sacred Wellness Advisor. She believes that abundance thrives in your ability to remain aligned and authentic, which is a daily practice. Mary has studied and practiced Yoga, Meditation and Reiki Energy Harmonizing for almost twenty years. By taking an intuitive approach, she focuses on creating a space for her clients to embody their true essence through Anchor Your Light Academy, an immersive experience available online or in Sedona, Arizona.

Mary is a #1 International Bestselling Author, Publisher and Speaker. She joyfully supports conscious coaches, thought leaders, visionaries, and entrepreneurs in becoming published authors and speakers by sharing their powerful story, message, and mission on a global platform. She has created a VIP experience that amplifies visibility, impact, and prosperity for her clients.

Website: www.marygooden.com
Facebook: https://www.facebook.com/mary.s.gooden

Amazon Author Page: https://www.amazon.com/author/marygooden

9
SARAH ALEX CARTER

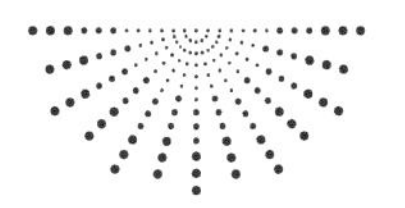

YOU ARE NOT ALONE

I paced back and forth, unable to sit down or stay still. I was extremely agitated, heart racing, sweat beading and palms wet. I felt like a caged wild animal. Not the ones you see at the zoo, who have resigned themselves to their fate behind a security fence, no, a wild animal that had just been caught in a trap. All wide eyed, full of fear and in a frenzy to escape. My breathing was quick and shallow, and I was on the verge of tears.

But these moments were not playing out in a dangerous situation where my life was threatened, nor was this part of a thrilling adventure where I was in a state of heightened excitement. In fact, I was in the reception of my doctor's surgery waiting to be called and seen for a routine appointment.

My name was called down the hallway, "Sarah Carter!" and I nervously made my way, shaking with anxiety, towards his open office door. I stepped in, sat down in front of the locum doctor and fell apart.

This is where my story starts, but to understand how I got to this point, we need to travel back 11 years.

In February 2006 our mother suddenly died. She was only 60 years old and her passing came as a huge shock to everyone who knew her. My mother, Jennifer, died of a PE or Pulmonary Embolism to the lungs. She was here one minute and gone the next. This devastating news created shockwaves through our family. Sadly, my mother's funeral was not the last I would attend that year and was followed by a succession of family members passing over a two-year period.

"The pain of grief is just as much part of life as the joy of love".

Grief is a strange process, and one I had not encountered before. I didn't know what to do with the tidal wave of emotions that kept hitting me. I was out of my depth and just as I came up for air, struggling and trying to gain control over the situation, another torrent of feelings would rise up and crash on me. It felt relentless. And so, instead of leaning into what was happening and processing all I was going through in a healthy, human way, I pushed the swirling, raging river of pain, hurt, disappointment and fear deep down within me. My inner defence mechanism kicked in and I went into autopilot.

I had always been fiercely independent and the Type A achiever in me found comfort in dealing with this sadness and turmoil by rising above it – I projected a cool, calm exterior. I got through every day with an Oscar-worthy performance of coping with everything coming my way. I returned to work, completed my Masters with Distinction, got a promotion, and pushed myself to excel in all I was doing.

And this strategy worked well. I appeared to be incredibly successful. From the outside looking in, I was doing brilliantly, and I imagined people saying in awe "Wow, Sarah's really got it together!". To be brutally honest, I got a kick out of managing these seismic shifts in life all by myself - I convinced myself I could handle all the proverbial as it hit the fan alone.

But then the cracks started to show. I got virus after virus. My skin broke out in cold sores. I ached and felt unwell. Bizarrely, I believed this was because I wasn't training my body enough, and so I started running and took on a 10K race. Then one day, 18 months after my mother's death, my body finally gave me a very clear warning that something wasn't right. I had my first panic attack.

One evening, after eating something that didn't agree with me, I was kneeling in the bathroom, vomiting. And when I got up, I felt a surge of pins and needles starting from my feet moving up towards my chest. It was overwhelming and I genuinely thought I was going to die. I thought my heart was going to stop and I would drop dead like my mother had. I ran to our bedroom where there was a full-length mirror – I looked at myself and told myself over and over "I am not going to die! I am not going to die!" My husband came rushing in and promptly called an ambulance. The paramedics arrived and I was hyperventilating, shaking, and not making any sense. They put an oxygen mask on me and spoke with my husband. They said I had experienced a panic attack and I would be OK. However, I did not feel OK. It was the most terrified I have ever been.

I gradually calmed down but was still shaking as a result of the adrenaline running through me. I was confused, scared, and didn't know what had just happened. Later that night I remember my husband lying in bed with me, holding me and telling me everything was going to be OK. I eventually fell asleep, exhausted by the ordeal.

The Body Never Lies

I woke up the following day with what I now know to be the biggest anxiety hangover ever. I felt ashamed, bewildered and still afraid. What had happened? Why did my body do that? What was wrong with me? I didn't have answers to the questions. And my body continued to behave strangely, rashes appeared on my skin, my hands seized up and I lost my appetite. The warning was clear – I was suffering from emotional pain on a physical level – but I didn't know this. And so, I did what I had practised in times of pain – I pushed the worry, fear, and anxiety down, deep down and kept on achieving!

Nearly a year later, whilst sitting in the cinema, I had pins and needles in my feet. And this triggered another massive panic attack. It happened again whilst out having a meal with friends. Then another in the cinema. And so, I started to fear these seemingly random attacks and became afraid of going to the cinema or out for a meal. The day after each episode, I felt the same shame and disappointment in myself. Unfortunately, during these early attacks I had no understanding of the physical changes in my body, no awareness of what fight or flight meant and absolutely no comprehension that my body was, in fact, trying to keep me safe. And to make matters worse, I also listened to wrong advice: "you don't need to have anything like CBT (Cognitive Behavioural Therapy)".

In 2010, I went for my then dream job – a full time lectureship at a university teaching fashion. At the same time, I fell pregnant, renovated our 1900's Welsh terrace and launched a side hustle exhibiting and selling my artwork. All these distractions abated my anxiety and gave me positive things to focus on, added to which I hadn't been to a funeral in a few years! However, in 2012, the stress of teaching full time, having a toddler and being bullied at my 'dream job' caught up with me. And again, the anxiety returned, looming over me like a menacing black cloud. It blotted out the blue sky, cast a gloom over everything and created a confusion in my mind, so disturbing, I was constantly afraid. At one point I thought I was schizophrenic!

And yet, I kept going, pushing, and achieving – alone. Hiding my panic and fear from everyone, including my husband. I acted as 'normal' as I could. I remember one time being in a meeting digging my nails into my palms to try and maintain my composure. The room was swimming, and I wasn't taking in anything being said, but I smiled and nodded, just as I had done many times before.

An Awful Charade

I mastered the art of this awful charade as I felt so ashamed of what was happening to me and believed I would be a burden on my family if they knew. I kept silent about my suffering because I saw it as a weakness. As a result, it was crushing me on the inside; my life as I knew it, carefree and easy, was slipping away and I honestly thought I would never be the same again. I felt incredibly lonely and afraid.

A new baby, new house, and another promotion later, my life seemed perfect. I had climbed the career ladder successfully and appeared to ‘have it all together’. And yet, in 2017, after years of hiding my anxiety, chronic stress and unhealed trauma, my body was too exhausted to go on and it started to display alarming physical reactions to this long-lived nightmare. Chest pains, palpitations, headaches, tinnitus, allergic reactions, slowed speech, dizziness, and weight loss were just some of the outward responses to my racing, anxious mind. It was as if a switch had been flipped and I could not turn it off, no matter how hard I tried. I found myself crying at meal times, unable to eat, and overwhelmed by the smallest of decisions. I had terrible brain fog and couldn’t concentrate. I would snap, shout, or become startled at any given moment – I was truly on edge.

This eventually tipped over into me staying in bed most of the day, unable to look after my children, becoming too weak to walk them to school or bathe them. I found simple, everyday tasks overwhelming. I didn’t brush my hair or look after myself. I was slowly disappearing. When I looked in the mirror, I saw a grey-faced, washed out shell of a person staring back, almost vacant, and hopeless. I eventually lost myself and my confidence hit rock bottom.

Hope is Born

But, in March 2017, after endless medical tests, examinations and scans, I met a doctor who would change my life forever. As I sat in front of this young man, I listed the symptoms I was experiencing. It was such a long list, I had written it into the notes on my phone to keep track of what was happening to me. I said with an earnest voice “these are all actually happening to me, I’m not imagining them!” I feared that he would think I was a hypochondriac. After a few more questions, reading my notes and assessing the clearly frightened patient in front of him, he gently suggested that what I was experiencing was anxiety and for me to think about taking medication to help alleviate my symptoms.

In that moment, it was as if the box I had kept myself in, with all my fears and emotions, was unlocked for the first time. A chink of light broke through the darkness and hope was born. This diagnosis was the permission I needed to face my pain and not hide from it any more. I could finally 'come out' of the anxiety closet and that brought a huge relief. It felt as if a weight had been lifted. I could talk to my family, share with them how I was feeling and I would no longer feel so alone. But, this diagnosis was also a double edged sword. As with any confirmation of an illness comes the decisions on how to heal and recover, and a choice as to what to do with this information. I wrestled with questions such as "would I have this label for the rest of my life?" and "if I go on medication, will I ever come off it?" My biggest fear was still "will I ever be the same again?"

I left the surgery lighter, but still unsure of whether I would take his advice of starting a course of antidepressants. It took a further week of misery to finally make the decision.

The Tide Begins to Turn

I remember the first time I felt the medication take effect. It was as though a blanket had been wrapped around my jittery nerves and I felt a calm I had not known in months. I slowly began to stay out of bed for longer periods, was able to eat and regain my strength and I started to see a change in my symptoms. This did not happen overnight, and it took months for my body to fully recover from the onslaught of cortisol and adrenaline, but the tide was beginning to turn. My mind was still prone to racing and catastrophizing. I still felt as though my thoughts and emotions were at war with me and I struggled to make sense of how I would function with my new diagnosis. "Would I always be anxious? How long would it take for me to feel 'normal' again?"

I was also relying on old behaviours - being fiercely independent, trying to control everything and being 'the best' at getting well - the very behaviours that had led to my breakdown in the first place. These entrenched ways of thinking and living were a barrier and I needed to strip away the old, to make way for new thinking and an altered perspective. I made a decision one day whilst I was writing in my journal. It was as if the heavens opened, angels sang and I had an epiphany. I was not going to be a victim anymore - I had a family and I wanted to deal with my demons so that they didn't have to live with them now or in the future. And then it dawned on me, like a bolt out of the blue: I needed to reach out and ask for help, I couldn't do this alone.

"Let me Hold That for You"

I had grown up an independent child, I would rarely ask for help and there were two reasons for this. I didn't want to be a burden to anyone, and I grew up with a single mother who also didn't ask for help when she needed it most. As nature and nurture played their role I learned over time that I would work it out and get by just fine on my own. Now, whilst this served me well in some ways - I travelled abroad, lived on my own, built a career - it also set me up for a very difficult time when the signs of stress and overwhelm started to show and I eventually broke down.

But with the realisation that I could not recover from this without the support of others, I had to learn to ask for help. There was an Everest in front of me - a mountain of historical hurt, pain, disappointment, judgement and fear. At the top of the mountain was a new vantage point, an open vista, but to get there, I needed a team of support. My first port of call was to the Mental Health Unit in my local hospital. I reached out, saw a therapist and joined a women's support group for those struggling with anxiety, depression and mental health illnesses. This led to many more lightbulb moments. I can clearly remember the visceral relief I felt when the therapist told me that everyone experiences the same symptoms of anxiety as I had in varying degrees - that I was not alone in what I was going through.

Next I sought help within my GP surgery from the counsellor from mental health charity MIND, who saw me for six weeks. Then, I dived deep into other sources of help through reading and learning from literature on anxiety, researching the medication I was taking and I finally started a self-led course of Cognitive Behavioural Therapy and Mindfulness Based Stress Reduction Therapy.

I turned to my family and friends for much needed daily support. My husband was there through it all, holding my hand, talking me through and wiping my tears when things got tough. Which they did. I never knew recovery was so hard and realised why so many choose to stay as they are. But for me the choice was clear, the pain of being a victim was greater than the struggle to overcome. I kept going. My sisters treated me to days out, helped with the children, shared their own struggles with me and we grew closer as a result. Friends listened to my endless voice notes of how I was feeling, invited me round for afternoon tea and kept reminding me that I was not alone. My willingness to now talk about my feelings allowed others to do the same, and they too told me they had similar experiences and were honest about their own health.

The final step I took was to pay for a private therapist. It was a big investment for me, but a year after my breakdown, I knew that there were doubts, fears and old baggage I was still carrying. I will never forget the reassurance and comfort I felt when I sat in his office and his words to me, when I told him I was still afraid, were "let me hold that for you".

Doing the Work

Over the past few years, I have looked at my behaviour, done a lot of work on myself and now recognise what has stopped me from asking for help. And the answer surprised me. It was fear and pride. Fear is what kept me holding on tight, unwilling to let go and reach out, as I was afraid I would be let down if I relied on someone else. And pride led me to believe that asking for help is a weakness, I was proud to struggle on and do it myself. That way I could never be disappointed. This potent mix of fear and pride kept me in a cycle of exhaustion, mistrust and resentment. It went something like this - I needed help, say with childcare, I wouldn't ask for help because I 'could do it all' and then, when I was too tired, frazzled and fed up I would berate myself for not being able to 'do it all'. And so, instead of reaching out to my husband, family and friends, I would strive even harder to prove I 'could do it all'! Madness, I know! I had become my own taskmaster and it was relentless.

And the price I paid for this independence was loneliness. An isolation that was all consuming. It started as a creeping feeling of doubt and was reinforced by my constant comparison to others. As my thinking became more blinkered and introspective, I stopped looking outward to others and this slowly turned into a vicious cycle of fear, shame and feeling like I was the only one experiencing any suffering.

Community and Compassion

So, how has this changed? What do I do differently now? Well, please be under no illusion - I am a work in progress. I still fall into the fear trap. And added to the fear is the well meaning thought of whether I am burdening someone else. 'But what if they're busy?' I ask, 'they have a lot going on in their lives already.' Or the fear may mingle with guilt, 'But it is my home/child/responsibility, I need to take care of this.' and the classic 'I'm sure I can fit it in' - whilst moving heaven and earth to actually fit it in! This final thought is the one that seals the deal - 'Other people manage, so why shouldn't I?'

But now, before I fall prey to this spiral of thoughts, I try to replace negative thinking with truth, this is slowly changing my perspective on reaching out to others. If I can remind myself of these truths, before my old default setting takes over, I will ask for help, share the load and not feel guilty or afraid.

There is a wonderful philosophy and phrase held by African culture called *ubuntu* which states that "I am because we are". This attitude and belief celebrates shared humanity and connects us universally. When we look up from our own pain and suffering and choose to share this with others, we are no longer alone. We also grant others the permission to do the same, and as a result, we come together as a community. I believe we were made for each other and when we look beyond ourselves and our limits, we experience a fuller, richer life.

And this is what I do with my clients as a wellbeing coach. I now support those who may feel alone in their experiences. This may be an executive at the top of their game who has little support as a result of their position and success. A busy working mum who feels isolated, juggling everything and trying to 'do it all' by herself. The perimenopausal woman who feels her symptoms are taking over her life and that she is losing herself as a result of hormonal change. Or the leader who wants to support their team but doesn't know how to get everyone on the same page.

Community and compassion are values I hold dear and these have been a lifeline in the midst of suffering, and enabled me to recover from pain. The truth that 'you are not alone and we can achieve more together' is now at the heart of how I live and lead in my life and business. Here are some of the other truths I remind myself and my clients of:

I am not a one man-band

One person trying to play every instrument never sounds good! So, put down the cymbals and drums and just focus on one thing at a time and allow others to play their part in your life.

People need people

The phrase 'it takes a village to raise a child' is true - and we all need each other. I am someone's child, sister, wife, mother, aunty, friend etc. We were intended to look to each other for support and help. If I believe in the power of community, then I need to embrace the help others can provide.

Communication is key

My recovery from burnout and breakdown started with a conversation. My wellness came through talking with others. Hope was born from honest communication. When you talk about your illness/struggles/limitations - they lose their power. The light of clear communication allows us to see the things that are hidden in the dark and acknowledge them for what they are.

Seek professional help

Talk with people who know, understand and have expertise and experience. Pick up the phone, search online, get referrals or recommendations from people you trust. There are professionals out there from doctors to coaches to therapists who can provide a safe space for you to learn more about yourself and your situation.

There is joy in helping

I get a lot of pleasure from helping others, and so, by asking for help, I am allowing others to feel that joy too. It becomes a two way relationship and the joy is doubled when shared.

Others don't do it all

Despite what you may see or assume - other people do ask for help. And they have different situations, lifestyles and relationships to me. All of these factor into how we live our lives and the support we experience.

Struggling is not a strength

I struggled on for years, full of ego and pride, and it made me miserable. It takes more strength and courage to ask for help than to go it alone. It may feel uncomfortable in the moment, but each time I reach out to others, I know it is a far better option in the long run.

I would like to be asked

If I knew someone was finding things tough or had a lot on their plate - I would want to be there for them and be someone they could lean on. Keep reminding yourself of that and think about the type of help you would like to receive.

My worth is not in doing

I am valuable because of who I am, not because of what I do. And so running myself ragged and spinning all of the plates all of the time doesn't make me a better person - it makes me an exhausted person!

Be the example

I want my family and friends to look to each other and know the importance of community, and so I model this behaviour and set a good example for them. I want my children to see that it is right and healthy to share responsibilities, to work as a team and know that their worth is not in doing it all.

Consider for yourself why you may find it difficult to get the support you need. Do you need to write your own set of truths that you can turn to and use to replace learned or negative thinking? I'd love to know, I mean, that's what I'm here for - to support you in your journey and keep the conversation going. Remember, you are not alone and we can achieve more together!

ABOUT THE AUTHOR

SARAH ALEX CARTER

Sarah Alex Carter is a Wellbeing Coach and Consultant who works with leaders who are struggling with stress, overwhelm and achieving an effective work/life balance. She offers specialist support and training on hormonal changes and the menopause. With her 1:1 coaching and group workshops she helps them to manage and prioritise their wellness together with navigating the challenges of leadership so that they can thrive in their role, support their staff, and achieve success. She is an award nominated wellbeing coach, certified in transformation coaching and has 20 years experience as a qualified teacher.

Sarah is the author of the self-development book *Upward: The Power of Looking Up*. Her articles on wellbeing and lifestyle have featured in international magazines and in her own blog via her website.

She lives in Wales, UK with her husband, two children and rescue Patterdale Terrier, Gwen.

Website: www.sarahalexcarter.com

Book: "Upward: The Power Of Looking Up"

Socials: @iamsarahalexcarter

10
ABOUT THE PUBLISHER

INSPIRED WORLD PUBLISHING AND DINA BEHRMAN

Inspired World Publishing was founded by former journalist-turned-PR strategist, Dina Behrman. It publishes multi-author books from entrepreneurs, changemakers and business leaders with a story to tell and expertise to share.

Dina works with entrepreneurs who want to inspire millions, skyrocket their visibility and attract more soulmate clients. She helps them stop being the internet's best kept secret, become the 'go to' expert and create a much bigger impact in the world by sharing their story and expertise in the press.

She launched her business following a decade working as a journalist, during which she was published in virtually every national UK newspaper and many magazines. She's worked as a publicist for a number of 6 and 7-figure industry leaders, and has also helped hundreds of entrepreneurs learn how to do their own

PR. She's been featured in Forbes, Entrepreneur, Huff Post, The Guardian, BBC radio, amongst others.

Find out more at www.dinabehrman.com.

Printed in France by Amazon
Brétigny-sur-Orge, FR